D1717063

EXPERIMENTS WITH

WITH

LIGHT

SCIENCE WHIZ
EXPERIMENTS

EXPERIMENTS WITH LIGHT

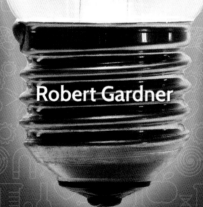

Robert Gardner

Enslow Publishing
101 W. 23rd Street
Suite 240
New York, NY 10011
USA
enslow.com

Published in 2018 by Enslow Publishing, LLC.
101 W. 23rd Street, Suite 240, New York, NY 10011

Library of Congress Cataloging-in-Publication Data

Names: Gardner, Robert, 1929- author.
Title: Experiments with light / Robert Gardner.
Description: New York, NY : Enslow Publishing, [2018] | Series: Science
    whiz experiments | Audience: 5-8.
Identifiers: LCCN 2016057788 | ISBN 9780766086807 (library bound ; alk. paper)
Subjects: LCSH: Light—Experiments—Juvenile literature.
Classification: LCC QC360 .G3675 2018 | DDC 535.078—dc23
LC record available at https://lccn.loc.gov/2016057788

Printed in China

To Our Readers: We have done our best to make sure all website addresses in this book were active and appropriate when we went to press. However, the author and the publisher have no control over and assume no liability for the material available on those websites or on any websites they may link to. Any comments or suggestions can be sent by e-mail to customerservice@enslow.com.

Illustrations by Joseph Hill

Photo Credits: Cover, p. 3, Christian Gstöttmayr/Moment/Getty Images; back cover and interior pages background pattern curiosity/Shutterstock.com.

Contents

Introduction

Life on planet Earth would not be possible without light. Sunlight heats our world and provides the energy plants need to make food. But what exactly is light? The behavior and properties of light are a fascinating branch of science called optics. Scientists who study light are physicists.

In this book, you will learn about light by doing experiments. Experimenting provides an understanding you cannot gain simply by reading. You will see that ordinary white light can be broken up into colors. You will find ways to mix (combine) those colored lights to form colors that will surprise you. You will learn how light can sometimes fool you. Things you think you see are not really there; they are mirages or illusions. You will discover how mirrors, lenses, and even pinholes form images, how light can be bent, reflected, polarized, absorbed, and much more. The beauty of experimenting with light is that you can literally see the results.

If you enjoy experimenting with light, you may want to continue learning about light by studying physics in high school and college. It could even become part of your life's work if you become a physicist, optician, optometrist, ophthalmologist, optical technician, or another occupation based on light.

At times, as you carry out the activities in this book, you may need a partner to help you. Try to work with someone who enjoys experimenting with light as much as you do. That way, you will both enjoy what you are doing. If any danger is involved in doing an experiment, it will be announced to you. **In some cases, to avoid danger, you will be asked to work with an adult. Please do so. Don't take any chances that could lead to an injury.**

Like any good scientist, you will find it useful to record ideas, notes, data, and anything you can conclude from your investigations in a notebook. This way you can keep track of the information you gather and the conclusions you reach. It will allow you to refer back to things you have done and help you in doing other projects in the future.

Entering a Science Fair

Some of the investigations in this book contain ideas you might use at a science fair. However, judges at science fairs do not reward projects or experiments that are simply copied from a book. For example, a diagram of the electromagnetic spectrum would not impress most judges; however, finding unique ways to measure the wavelength of light or the energy of different wavelengths would certainly attract their attention.

Science fair judges tend to reward creative thought and imagination. It is difficult to be creative or imaginative unless you are really interested in your project, so try to choose an investigation that appeals to you. Before you jump into a project, consider, too, your own talents and the cost of the materials you will need.

If you decide to use an experiment or idea found in this book for a science fair, you should modify or extend it. This should not be difficult because you will discover as you carry out investigations, new ideas come to mind. Ideas will come to you that could make excellent science fair projects, particularly because the ideas are your own and are interesting to you.

If you decide to enter a science fair and have never done so, you should read some of the books listed in the Further Reading section. These books deal specifically with science fairs and will provide plenty of hints and useful information that will help you to avoid the problems that first-time entrants sometimes experience. You'll learn how to prepare appealing reports that include charts and graphs, how to set up and display your work, how to present your project, and how to relate to judges and visitors.

Be Safe

Most of the projects included in this book are very safe. However, the following safety rules are well worth reading before you start any project.

1. **Never look directly at the sun! It can damage your eyes.**
2. Do any experiments or projects, whether from this book or of your own design, **under the supervision of a science teacher or other knowledgeable adult**.
3. Read all instructions carefully before beginning a project. If you have questions, check with your supervisor before going any further.
4. Maintain a serious attitude while conducting experiments. Fooling around can be dangerous to you and to others.
5. Wear approved safety goggles when you are working with a flame or doing anything that might injure your eyes.
6. Have a first aid kit nearby while you are experimenting.
7. Do not put your fingers or any object other than properly designed electrical connectors into electrical outlets.
8. Never let water droplets come in contact with a hot light bulb.
9. Never experiment with household electricity.

Following the Scientific Method

Scientists look at the world and try to understand how things work. They make careful observations and conduct research. Different areas of science use different approaches. Depending on the problem, one method is likely to be better than another. Designing a new medicine for heart disease, studying the spread of an invasive plant such as purple loosestrife, and finding evidence of water on Mars all require different methods.

Despite the differences, all scientists use a similar general approach in doing experiments. This is called the scientific method. In most experiments, some or all of the following steps are used: observing a problem, formulating a question, making a hypothesis (an answer to the question), making a prediction (an if-then statement), designing and conducting an experiment, analyzing results, drawing conclusions, and accepting or rejecting the hypothesis. Scientists then share their findings by writing articles that are published.

You might wonder how to start an experiment. When you observe something, you may become curious and ask a question. Your question, which could arise from an earlier experiment or from reading, may be answered by a well-designed investigation. Once you have a question, you can make a hypothesis. Your hypothesis is a possible answer to the question. Once you have a hypothesis, it is time to design an experiment to test a consequence of your hypothesis.

In most cases you should do a controlled experiment. This means having two groups that are treated the same except for the one factor being tested. That factor is called a variable. For example, suppose your question is "Do green plants need light?" Your hypothesis might be that they do need light. To test the hypothesis, you would use two groups of green plants. One group is called the control group, the other is called the experimental group. The two groups should be treated the same except for one factor. Both should be planted in the same amount and type of soil, given the same amount of water, kept at the same temperature, and so forth. The control group would be placed in the dark. The experimental group would be put in the light. Light is the variable. It is the only difference between the two groups.

During the experiment, you would collect data. For example, you might measure the plants' growth in centimeters, count the number of living and dead leaves, and note the color and condition of the leaves. By comparing the data collected from the control and experimental groups over a few weeks, you would draw conclusions. Healthier growth and survival rates of plants grown in light would allow you to conclude that green plants need light.

Two other terms are often used in scientific experiments—dependent and independent variables. One dependent variable in this example is healthy growth, which depends on light being present. Light is the independent variable. It doesn't depend on anything.

After the data are collected, they are analyzed to see if they support or reject the hypothesis. The results of one experiment often lead you to a related question. Or they may send you off in a different direction. Whatever the results, something can be learned from every experiment.

Chapter 1

Sources and Paths of Light

Sunlight helps us see, and it also provides the heat we need to live and the energy plants need to photosynthesize. Without the energy that sunlight provides, there would be no life on Earth.

But there are other sources of light—stars, light bulbs, fires, chemical reactions, even fireflies and some deep-sea fish. The light from an ordinary light bulb (not a fluorescent light) actually comes from the hot filament. The filament is a hot metal (tungsten), so you see that hot metals are also a source of light.

You might wonder why the moon has not been mentioned. The reason is that moonlight is actually sunlight that has been reflected from the moon's surface.

1.1 What Is Light's Normal Path?

Have you ever seen a carpenter look down a board to see if it is straight? The carpenter assumes that light travels in straight lines. But does light really travel in straight lines? You can find out by doing an experiment.

1. Make a stack of three index cards. Use a paper punch to punch a hole in all three cards at the same time. By holding the cards together, all the holes will be at the same place on each card. See Figure 1 to get an idea of where to punch the hole.

2. Using tape, fasten each card to a wooden block. Be sure the bottom edge of each card touches the bottom edge of each block. Place the cards on a table near a window, about 50 cm (20 in) apart. Look through the hole in one card. Move the second card so that the light from the window passes through it as well as the card you are looking through. Finally, ask a partner to move the third card until you can see light from the window through all three holes.

3. Cut a piece of string about 2 m (2 yds) long. Being careful not to move the cards, thread the string through all three holes.

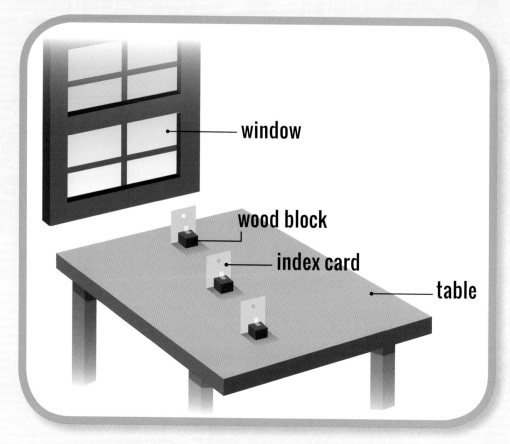

Figure 1. You can find the path that light follows.

Have your partner hold one end of the string while you hold the other. Carefully tighten the string. Do the holes lie along a straight line?

To reach your eye, light from the window must have passed through all three holes.

4. Darken the room. Hold a flashlight in front of the hole in the card you looked through. Ask a partner to hold a piece of paper beyond the third index card. Can you see a circle of light on the paper? What does this tell you about the path followed by the light?

1.2 Light in Straight Paths

Figure 2a shows light rays (very narrow beams of light) coming from a bright object. If the rays pass through a tiny hole in straight lines, they should produce an upside-down image of the object on a screen on the other side of the small opening. Can light traveling through a pinhole produce such an image? If it can, you have more evidence that light travels in straight lines.

1. Put a candle on a counter or table. Place a box in front of the candle as shown in Figure 2b.

2. Cut a square hole in the box. Make the square about 2.5 cm (1 in) on a side. The hole should be about the same height above the table as the candle's wick. Tape a piece of black construction paper over the hole. Use a large pin, such as a T-pin or hat pin, to make a hole in the paper.

3. Make a light screen by taping a sheet of white paper to a piece of cardboard.

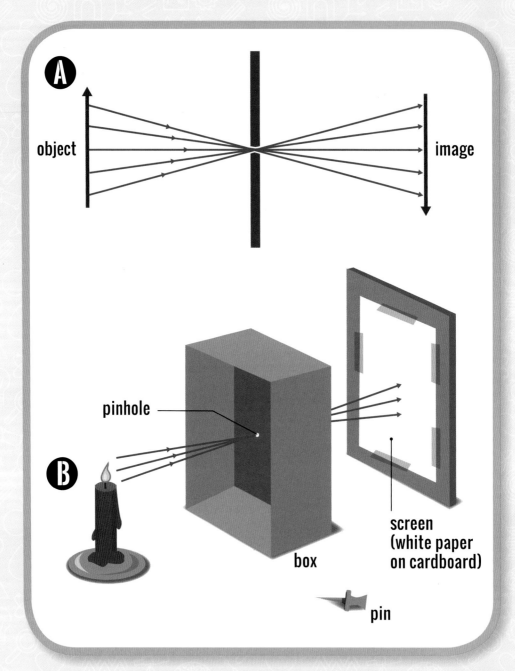

A

object   image

B

pinhole

screen
(white paper
on cardboard)

box

pin

Figure 2. a) A pinhole can be used to produce an image. Shown are a few of the many light rays that form the image. The arrows show the direction of the light rays. b) Can you make a pinhole image of a candle's flame?

4. Darken the room. **Ask an adult** to light the candle. The only light should be the candle flame. Hold the screen near the pinhole on the side opposite the candle flame.

   Can you see an image of the candle flame on the white paper screen? Is the image upside down? What happens to the size of the image as you move the screen closer to the pinhole? What happens to the size of the image when you move the screen farther from the pinhole? Look carefully at Figure 2a. Can you explain why the size of the image changes as you move the screen closer to or farther from the pinhole?

5. Place the screen so it is the same distance from the pinhole as the candle. Does the length of the image appear to be about the same as the length of the flame? Do you think it should be the same size? Why?

6. Use scissors to cut a square hole in an index card. Make the hole about 2.5 cm (1 in) on a side. Tape a piece of aluminum foil over the hole.

7. Place the card, foil down, on a piece of cardboard. Use a T-pin or sewing needle to punch a hole in the center of the foil.

8. Place a low-wattage light bulb (15–30 watts) in a socket. Turn on the light bulb. Move the pinhole close to the writing on the bulb. Hold your eye close to the pinhole. Why do you see a magnified image of the print on the bulb?

   Can you use the pinhole to magnify small print when viewed in bright light?

9. Make a pinhole by pushing together the tips of your index fingers and thumbs of both hands. Can you use this pinhole to magnify print? Can it be used to see distant objects better?

On a bright sunny day, look at the circles of light (sun dapples) that appear in the shade of a leafy tree. What do you think causes these circles? What experiment could you do to help confirm your explanation (hypothesis)?

You can build a pinhole camera, which uses a pinhole in place of a lens. Such a camera can take photographs of stationary objects even in dim light. Why can't such a camera be used for action photos that require a short exposure?

1.3 The Law of Reflection

On a sunny day take a mirror outside. **(Do not look directly at the sun. It can damage your eyes.)** Use the mirror to redirect the sunlight onto the side of a building, the ground, a tree, a car, but not onto a person. (Instead of the sun, you can use a light bulb in a dark or dimly lighted room.) The redirection of light by a mirror is called reflection. Every time you look into a mirror, you are seeing light that has been reflected from your face. But how is light reflected? You can answer that question by doing an experiment.

1. Lay a sheet of cardboard about 30 cm (12 inches) square on a counter or table. Put a sheet of white paper on the cardboard.

2. Use a piece of clay to stand a mirror near one side of the paper. If possible, use a mirror that reflects light from its front surface. To see if a mirror has a front-reflecting surface, put your fingertip against the mirror. If your fingertip is touching the image of your fingertip, it is a front surface mirror. If there is a gap between your fingertip and its image, reflection is from the mirror's rear surface.

3. If you are using a front surface mirror, use a sharp pencil to draw a line on the paper along the mirror's front surface;

otherwise, draw a line along its rear surface. Should the mirror be moved, the line will allow you to put the mirror back where it was.

4. Stick two straight pins through the paper and into the cardboard as shown in Figure 3a. Call these the object pins. An imaginary line connecting the object pins and the mirror should be at an angle to the mirror's surface. The two pins define a light ray traveling to the mirror.

5. Move your head to the other side of the mirror. Look at the reflected light coming from the two pins, which is the mirror images of the two pins.

6. Use two more pins to map the path of the reflected light ray. To do this, line up these pins with the images of the two pins that you see in the mirror (Figure 3b). Stick these two pins into the cardboard. Call these the image pins.

7. Remove the mirror. Use a ruler to draw a line connecting the object pins to the line you drew along the mirror's reflecting surface. Then draw a line connecting the image pins to the same line (Figure 3c). As you can see, the lines meet, or nearly meet, at the mirror's reflecting surface. (If you have a mirror with a rear-reflecting surface, the lines will probably meet slightly in front of the surface. You will see why in a later experiment.)

   The line you drew along the object pins to the mirror represents what is called an incident ray (a ray that comes to the mirror). The line you drew along the image pins to the mirror represents what is called a reflected ray (a ray that leaves the mirror).

8. Use a protractor to measure the angle between the incident ray and an imaginary line perpendicular to the mirror (Figure 3d), which is called the normal. This angle is called the angle of incidence (i).

9. In the same way, measure the angle between the reflected ray and a line perpendicular to the mirror. This angle is called the angle of reflection (r). How do these two angles compare? Are they equal or nearly so?

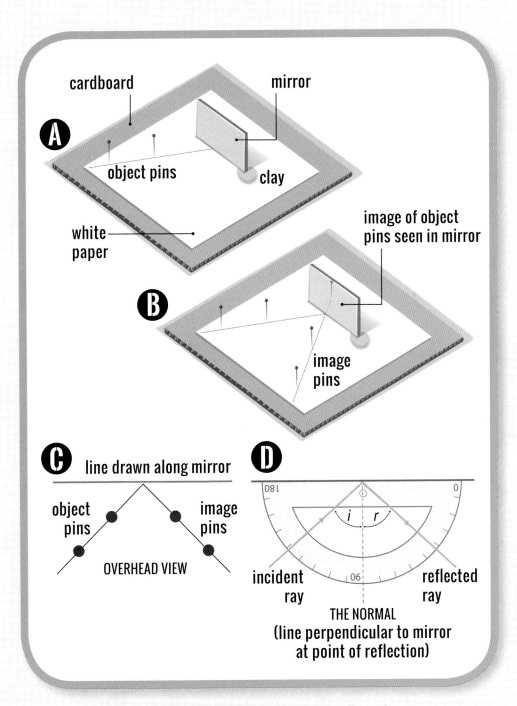

Figure 3. You can make incident and reflected rays and measure their angles.

10. Using the same materials, compare the angles of incidence and reflection for a number of different angles of incidence. Based on your data, how would you express a law about the reflection of light from a smooth, plane (flat) surface?

Here is the law of reflection as stated by physicists: The angle of reflection equals the angle of incidence and lies on the other side of the normal (a line perpendicular to the mirror at the point of reflection). The incident and reflected rays are on the same plane.

1.4 A Mirror Image

In the previous experiment, you saw the images of the object pins when you looked into the mirror. You see your own image when you look into a mirror. But where are the images you see? To find out, you can do several experiments.

1. To begin, place a mirror near the center of a sheet of white paper resting on a piece of cardboard. Stand a pencil upright about 10 cm (4 in) in front of the mirror. Small lumps of clay can be used to support the mirror and the pencil. Draw a line along the front or rear of the mirror so you will know where it stood after it is removed.

2. Locate one reflected ray from the pencil by lining up two pins with the pencil's image in the mirror. Use two more pins to locate a second ray from the pencil as shown in Figure 4a. Since both rays seem to be coming from the image, the point where they meet should be the position of the image.

3. Remove the mirror and use a ruler to extend those two rays until they meet as shown in Figure 4b. Where is the image of the pencil located? How does its distance from the mirror compare with the distance of the object (pencil) from the mirror?

4. Repeat the experiment several times with the pencil at different distances in front of the mirror. For each

experiment, how does the distance of the image from the mirror compare with the distance of the object (pencil) from the mirror?

5. Another way to locate an image is by use of a technique called parallax. It involves looking at an image from different angles. To see how it works, hold one finger at arm's length in front of your face. Hold the other finger close to your face. Now look at both fingers, first with your right eye, then with your left eye. As you can see, the position of the near finger seems to shift relative to the distant finger.

6. Now hold one finger directly under the other at arm's length. Again, close first one eye and then the other. This time the two fingers do not shift relative to one another. We say there is no parallax between them. (But notice that there is parallax between the two fingers and an object across the room.)

7. Lack of parallax can be used to locate the image you see in a mirror. Hold a second pencil behind the mirror as shown in Figure 4c. Put your head behind the pencil in front of the mirror. You can see the entire pencil in front of the mirror, its image in the mirror, and the top of the second pencil behind the mirror.

8. Move the pencil behind the mirror to different positions keeping it in line with the image of the pencil in front of the mirror. At each position, look first with your right eye and then with your left eye. Keep moving the pencil until there is no parallax between the image and the pencil you are moving behind the mirror. When the image and the pencil stick together no matter with which eye you view them, you know the pencil behind the mirror is at the same place as the image of the pencil you see in the mirror.

9. Measure the distance from the mirror to the pencil in front of the mirror. Then measure the distance from the mirror to the pencil behind the mirror (the position of the image). How do these distances compare?

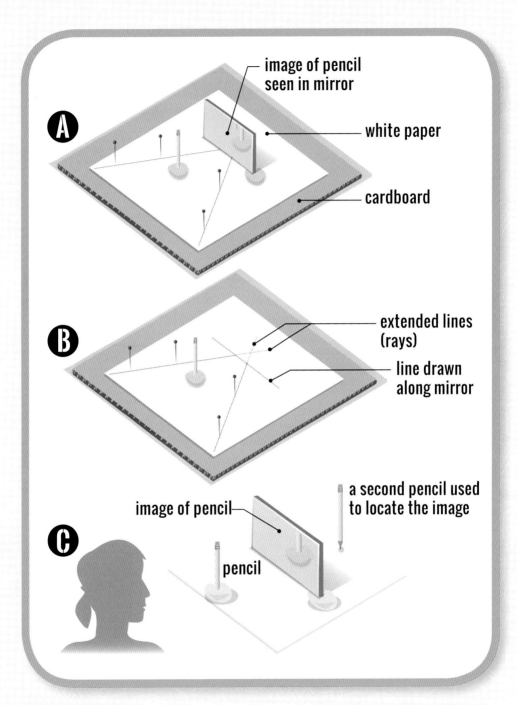

Figure 4. You can locate the image seen in a mirror by finding where reflected rays seem to come from (a, b) or by lack of parallax (c).

10. Repeat the experiment several times with the pencil at different distances from the mirror. What can you conclude about the apparent location of the pencil's image? What does this experiment lead you to conclude? What is the location of your image when you look into a plane mirror?

1.5 More Mirror Images

1. Prepare a two-slit frame that will enable you to produce two light "rays." You can make the frame using popsicle sticks. Use only sticks that are very straight to make the frame as shown in Figure 5a. Use the inside corner of a box to align the first two sticks. A small drop of glue at points where the sticks overlap will bind them together very well. Glue a straight popsicle stick across the center of the frame. Add another straight popsicle stick to each side of the center stick. Leave a slit about 1 mm wide on either side of the center stick as shown in Figure 5a.

2. Cover the openings that remain with black construction paper you can tape to the frame (Figure 5b).

3. Place the two-slit frame on white paper that rests on a sheet of cardboard as shown in Figure 5c. A small lump of clay can be used to keep the frame upright.

4. Use a clear 60-watt light bulb with a straight-line filament to send light through the two slits. The light bulb's filament

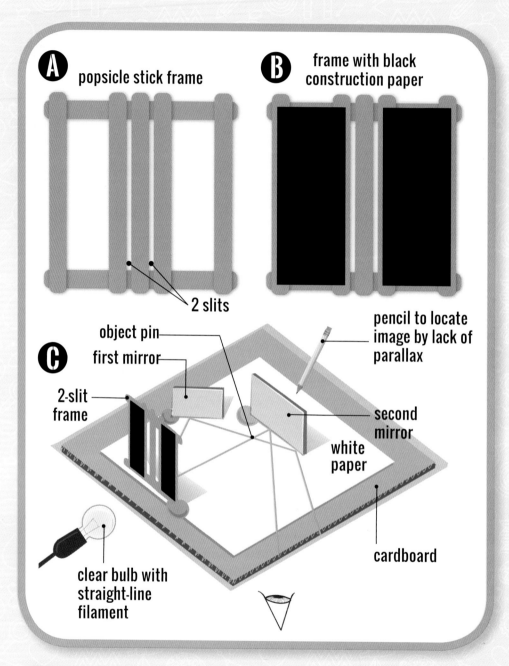

A popsicle stick frame

B frame with black construction paper

2 slits

C

object pin

first mirror

2-slit frame

pencil to locate image by lack of parallax

second mirror

white paper

cardboard

clear bulb with straight-line filament

Figure 5. a) Make a two-slit frame. b) Cover the rest of the frame with black paper. c) A model shows how an image is produced by a plane mirror.

should be vertical as shown in Figure 5c. Use a small mirror to reflect one of the rays so that it crosses the other ray. Let the point where the two rays cross represent a point on an object. Stick a small pin into that point.

5. Use a second mirror to reflect the rays that travel from the "object." Look into that second mirror. You will see the pin's image. You will also see the reflected rays that seem to be coming from the image of the object point. Where does the image of the object appear to be?

   To confirm that the image of the pin and point of light are where you think they are, locate the image with a pencil and lack of parallax. Save your two-slit frame. You can use it for other experiments in this book.

Try This for Fun

- **Have an adult** light a short candle in a dark room. Place the candle several centimeters in front of an upright pane of clear glass. Then place a large jar of water behind the glass so that the image of the burning candle appears to be in the jar of water. By hiding the candle with a screen, can you convince someone that the candle is burning underwater?

1.6 Reflected Light Through Water

THINGS YOU WILL NEED:

- sheet of cardboard about 30 cm (12 in) square
- white paper
- clear container about 12 cm (5 in) long x 6 cm (2.5 in) wide x 5 cm (2 in) deep
- water
- small mirror
- masking tape
- straight pins
- pencil
- ruler
- laser pointer (or large comb and flashlight)
- milk

If you did Experiment 1.3 with the mirror immersed in water, do you think the results would be different?

1. To find out, cover a sheet of cardboard with white paper. Place a clear, rectangular, plastic container like the one shown in Figure 6a on the paper. Nearly fill the container with water. Put a mirror in the water against one long side of the container. If part of the mirror is above the water, cover that part with masking tape. That way only light that goes though water will be reflected.

2. Proceed in the same way you did in Experiment 1.3. Stick two straight pins through the paper and into the cardboard as shown in Figure 6a. Call these the object pins. An imaginary line connecting the object pins should be at an angle to the mirror's surface.

3. Move your head to the other side of the paper and look at the reflected light coming from the two pins; that is, the images of the two pins. Use two more pins (the image pins) to map

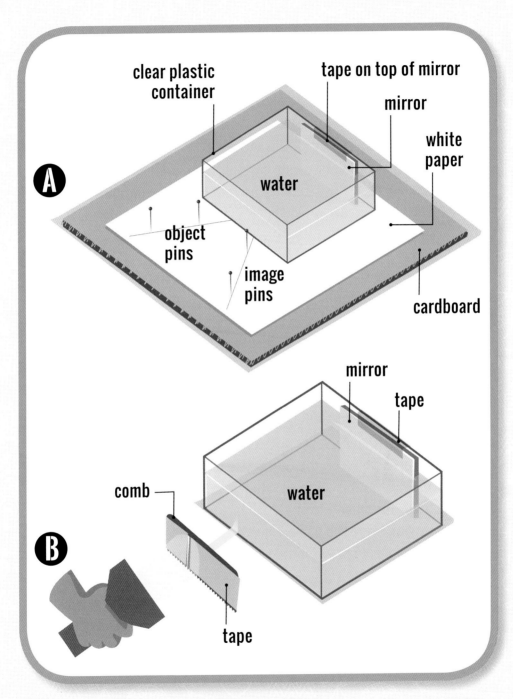

Figure 6. a) Will anything be different if light is reflected in water? b) What happens to light when it passes from air into water?

the path of the reflected light ray. Line up these pins with the images of the two pins that you see in the mirror. Stick these two pins into the cardboard.

4. Use a pencil to draw a line along the back of the mirror. (The line will actually be the thickness of the container wall behind the mirror.)

5. Remove the container, being careful not to spill any water. Use a ruler to extend the incident and reflected rays defined by the pins.

As you can see, the rays do not meet at the mirror as they did in Experiment 1.3. They meet well in front of the mirror. But how can this be? There is nothing in the water to reflect the rays. Can you suggest a hypothesis to explain what you have observed?

Let's look more closely at what happens when light passes from air into water.

6. If you have a laser pointer, **under adult supervision** shine the laser beam into the water at the same angle as the incident ray defined by the two pins.

7. If you do not have a laser pointer, find a large comb with fairly wide spaces between the teeth. Use tape to cover all but one space between the comb's teeth. Hold the comb with one hand. Use your other hand to shine a flashlight through the opening (Figure 6b). Have the narrow beam strike the water at about the same angle as the ray defined by the two incident pins.

If you have difficulty seeing the beam clearly, add a few drops of milk to the water and stir. Then try shining the laser beam or the flashlight again.

What happens to light as it passes from air into water? How does this explain why the light rays that were reflected in water did not meet at the mirror as they did in Experiment 1.3?

1.7 A Look at Refraction

As you saw in the previous experiment, light bends (is refracted) when it enters water at an angle. You can compare the angle of incidence of a light ray approaching a liquid with the angle of refraction of the same ray after entering the liquid (see Figure 7a).

1. Lay a sheet of white paper on a cardboard sheet. Place a clear, rectangular, container near the center of the paper. Nearly fill the container with water. With a sharp pencil, mark the sides of the container on the paper.

2. Use two pins to define an incident ray to the water as shown in Figure 7a.

3. Go to the other side of the container. Line up two more pins with the two that you placed on the opposite side of the container by looking through the water toward the first two pins.

4. Carefully remove the container of water. Use a ruler to draw the two light rays defined by the pins. You can probably see that the two rays are parallel but not in line with one another. Light entering the water is bent (refracted) toward the normal (a line perpendicular to the water at the point

the light enters the water). It is refracted away from the normal by the same amount when it leaves the water and enters air.

We know that light travels in straight lines. Therefore, the path that the light must have followed in the water is the line connecting the points where it entered and left the water.

5. Draw that ray on the paper. Use a protractor to measure the angles of incidence and refraction as shown in Figure 7b. How do they compare? What is the ratio of angle *i* to angle *r* (*i*/*r*)?

6. Repeat the experiment for a number of different angles of incidence. Try to go from angles of about 20 degrees to 80 degrees. You may find it hard to see the incident pins through the water at large angles of incidence. Do the best you can. Is the ratio of angle *i* to angle *r* constant, or does it change as the angle of incidence grows larger?

As you have seen, light bends toward the normal when it enters water and away from the normal when it passes from water into air. Suppose you were to gradually increase the angle of a light beam going from water into air. Eventually, the beam would leave the water at an angle of 90 degrees. What would happen if you increased the angle a little more?

7. To find out, add a pinch of non-dairy creamer to a clear, deep, water-filled, plastic container. Stir to spread the creamer throughout the water. Then, **under adult supervision**, shine a laser pointer into the cloudy water as shown in Figure 7c. What happens when the angle of the beam in the water approaches 49 degrees?

At 48.8 degrees, all the light is reflected. None of the light leaves the water and enters the air. This is known as total internal reflection and 48.8 degrees is called the critical angle for light passing from water into air.

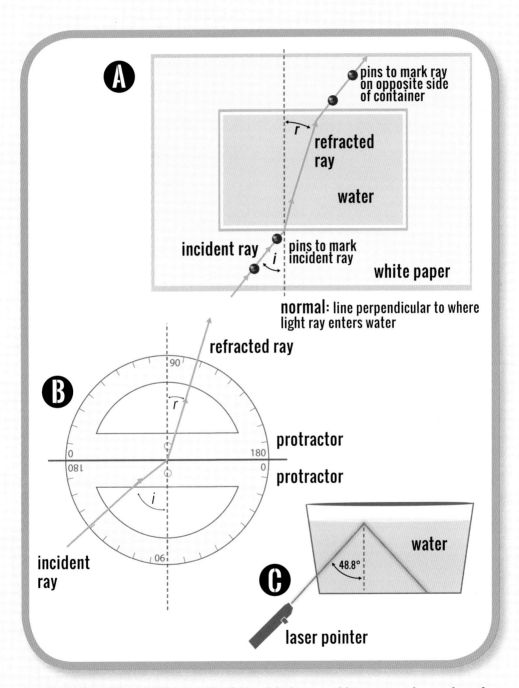

Figure 7. a) Trace incident and refracted light rays. b) Measure the angles of incidence *(i)* and refraction *(r)*. c) Find the critical angle for light passing from water into air.

Try This for Fun

- Put a coin in an empty mug that isn't clear. Lower your line of sight until the coin just disappears below the rim of the mug. Pour water slowly into the mug. The coin will come back into view. Can you explain why?

- Put the lower half of a pencil in a glass of water. When you look at it from a certain angle, it looks as if it is broken. Can you explain why?

Under adult supervision, try doing Experiment 1.7 using a laser pointer or a narrow beam of light rather than pins.

Repeat the experiment using rubbing alcohol, clear cooking oil, mineral oil, and clear glass or plastic in place of water. Do any of these materials refract light more or less than water?

What is Snell's law? Do the results of your experiment confirm Snell's law?

1.8 A Disappearing Glass

1. Find some transparent plastic tape. Be careful, some plastic tape is not clear. The clear tape refracts light by just about the same amount as clear or light-colored cooking oil.

2. Pour some clear cooking oil into a clean glass or beaker. Then dip one end of the transparent plastic tape into the oil. What happens to the visibility of the end of the tape submerged in the oil?

3. If you have a glass stirring rod, or can borrow one from your school's science lab, put the stirring rod in the clear cooking oil. The oil bends light the same (or nearly the same) amount as the glass rod. The bottom of the stirring rod will disappear. If the glass and liquid don't have exactly the same refractivity, you'll be able to see the submerged glass rod by looking closely. You might try a clear drinking straw in place of the glass rod.

The tape and glass disappeared in the oil because they all refract light by about the same amount. As far as light is concerned, the materials are the same. Therefore, light is not reflected or refracted as it passes from oil to glass or tape. Since objects are visible only when they reflect light to our eyes, the tape and glass become invisible (or nearly so) when in cooking oil.

Try This for Fun

- Tell your friends you can make things disappear. Then lower a small Pyrex glass beaker into a clear container that holds clear or light-colored cooking oil.

1.9 White Light and Colored Light

1. Cover one of the slits in the two-slit frame you made for Experiment 1.5 with a strip of black construction paper. Use tape to secure it to the frame. Use a lump of clay to stand the frame upright.

2. Darken the room and turn on a clear light bulb that has a straight-line filament. The filament should be vertical so that it is parallel to the narrow slit as shown in Figure 8. The light should be far enough from the slit so that a narrow beam of light is formed by the slit.

3. Lay a sheet of white paper in front of the slit. Place a small, clear, rectangular or square plastic container on the narrow light beam coming through the slit. Add water to the container until it is nearly full. You could also use a glass or plastic block or make one by placing a stack of microscope slides side by side.

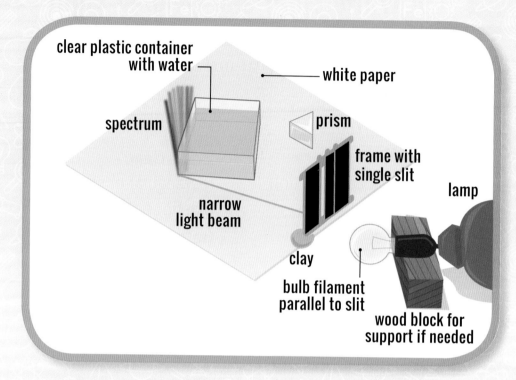

Figure 8. Refracted light, if bent sharply, can produce a spectrum.

4. Turn the container or glass block so that the light hits the box or block at a sharp angle as shown in Figure 8. Notice how the light is bent (refracted) as it enters and leaves the water or block. If you bend the light enough, you can turn the refracted beam into a band of colors—a spectrum. Look carefully at the colors. Which color is refracted the most? The least? The spreading of the refracted light into different colors is called dispersion. Where have you seen dispersion in the natural world?

5. Replace the container of water with a glass or plastic prism. You will find that you can cause dispersion by placing the prism on the light beam.

On a sunny day, take the prism outside. Turn it about in the sunlight until you produce a spectrum on the side of a building. How is this spectrum similar to the one you produced inside? How is it different?

Chapter 2

A Look at Light and Lenses

If you have ever visited an observatory and looked through a telescope, you have seen how lenses and mirrors can make something far away appear larger. The telescope takes advantage of the behavior of light to allow us to view objects in the night sky.

Lenses and mirrors are tools that bend light. There are different types and shapes of lenses and mirrors. In this chapter you will investigate lenses. Lenses form images by refracting light. You will also study curved mirrors, which form images by reflecting light.

Making models of these lenses will help you to see how they work. You will find that an object's image may be real or virtual, right-side up or upside down. It may be magnified or diminished in size compared to the object. Before you do the experiments in this chapter, there is something you need to know about the light rays from distant objects. Experiment 2.1 will provide that knowledge.

2.1 Light Rays from Far Away

THINGS YOU WILL NEED:

- cardboard
- white paper
- pins
- clear 60-watt light bulb with straight-line filament
- socket for light bulb
- magnifying glass (convex lens)
- facial tissue
- light-colored wall opposite a window
- ruler
- notebook
- pen or pencil
- tubular showcase bulb
- dark room
- scissors
- tissue paper

1. Cover a sheet of cardboard with white paper. Insert three pins side by side and about 3–4 cm (1.5 in) apart near one side of the cardboard as shown in Figure 9a.

2. Hold the cardboard and pins near a point of light. Use the end of a straight-line filament in a clear 60-watt light bulb as your light source. When viewed from the end of the filament, it is a point source of light.

3. Look at the shadows cast by the pins. The shadows show you that the light rays from the light are traveling outward like radii from a point at the center of a circle.

4. Slowly move the cardboard away from the light. What happens to the shadows? Look at the shadows again when you are several feet from the light. Are the shadows very nearly parallel?

     As you can see, light rays from distant objects are essentially parallel. Now you will see how parallel light rays can help you

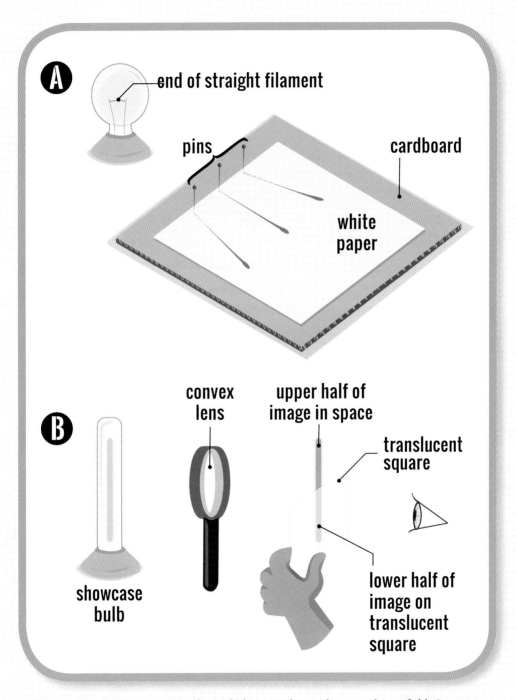

A end of straight filament

pins

cardboard

white paper

B convex lens

upper half of image in space

translucent square

showcase bulb

lower half of image on translucent square

Figure 9. a) What is true about light rays from distant objects? b) Can you confirm that an image is real?

determine the focal length of a lens. If you have a magnifying glass, you have a convex lens. Convex lenses are fat in the middle and thinner at the edges.

5. Cover your fingers with a facial tissue and feel the lens. Can you tell that the middle of the lens is thicker than the edges?

6. Hold a convex lens, such as a magnifying glass, near a light-colored wall opposite a window. Use the lens to make an image on the wall of the scene you see through the window. To do this, move the lens closer and farther from the wall until you obtain a clear image of the scene. What do you notice about the image?

As you see, this image is real. It is really on the wall. The images you saw in a plane mirror in Experiment 1.4 were virtual images formed by reflected light rays that seem to be coming from behind the mirror. Real images are formed by light rays that really do come together. Real images can be "captured" on a screen; virtual images cannot.

7. Keep the lens at a point where the image is sharp. Use a ruler to measure the distance from the image on the wall to the center of the lens. Record that distance. It is the focal length of the lens.

Since the image is formed by light from distant objects, the rays from those objects are essentially parallel when they reach the lens. The focal length of a convex lens is distance from the center of the lens to the focal point—the point where parallel rays are brought together. Every point on the image was formed from parallel rays that came from every point on the objects seen in the image. Therefore, the distance you recorded is the focal length of the lens. You will use the focal length in the next experiment.

8. To confirm the reality of such images, place a tubular showcase bulb in a socket. Turn on the bulb in a dark room.

9. Use scissors to cut an 8-cm (3-in) square from a piece of tissue paper.

10. Hold the square with one hand. Hold a convex lens in the other. Move the lens and paper until you capture the image of the bulb's long filament on the paper. Place your eye so that you see the top half of the image above the paper as shown in Figure 9b. The lower half of the image is on the paper. Use parallax to prove that the two halves of the image are at the same place. Move your head slightly to the right and left. You will see that the two halves of the image "stick" together.

Try This for Fun

- Hold a clear glass marble close to a wall opposite a window. A tiny image can be seen on the wall. Can you explain why?

- Place a single drop of water on the print of a glossy magazine. The print will be magnified. Can you explain why?

IDEAS FOR A SCIENCE FAIR PROJECT

- Use two convex lenses to make a simple microscope. Can you use two more to make a simple telescope?

- Obtain a concave lens. How does it refract light? What kind of images does it produce?

- How are convex and concave lenses used to make eyeglasses that compensate for nearsightedness and farsightedness?

2.2 **The Science of a Convex Lens**

You can make a model of a convex lens. The model will help you to see how a lens refracts light to make images.

1. Put a clear light bulb with a straight-line filament in a socket. Be sure the filament is vertical. Place the two-slit frame you used in Experiment 1.5 a few centimeters (inches) from the light bulb. A lump of clay can be used to support the frame. Lay a long sheet of white paper beyond the frame.

2. Darken the room and turn on the light bulb. You should see two narrow beams of light beyond the two slits as shown in Figure 10a. Put a jar of water on the two narrow light beams coming through the slits. The jar of water is a two-dimensional convex lens. What happens to the light rays as they enter and leave the lens?

3. You can make an even better model to show how a lens forms an image. Use a plane mirror to reflect one of the rays so that it crosses the other ray as shown in Figure 10b. The point where the two rays cross can represent a point on an object. The two rays coming from that point can represent two rays of light coming from a point on an object.

4. Place the jar of water so that the two rays enter the lens. As you will see, the two rays are brought together to form a point on the other side of the lens. That point represents a point on the image formed by the lens.

5. Move the lens a little closer to the point representing the object. What happens to the distance between the image and the lens?

6. Slowly move the lens closer to the "object." At some point, you will find that the rays coming from the lens are parallel. What happens if you move the lens still closer to the "object"?

7. To see many rays of light refracted by a lens, replace the two-slit frame with a large comb or hair pick. Place the lens several centimeters (inches) in front of the comb. Notice how the rays are bent as they enter and leave the lens.

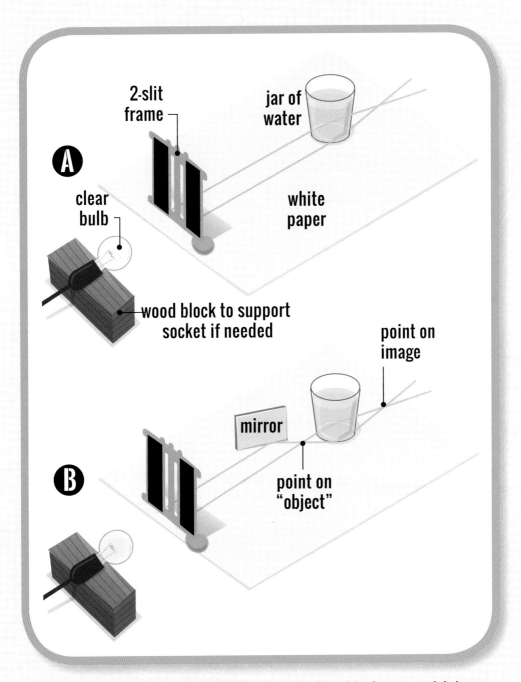

Figure 10. a) You can make a model of a convex lens. b) A better model shows how one point on an object becomes one point on an image.

Try This for Fun

- Remove a "one-eyed" jack (Jack of spades or Jack of hearts) from a deck of cards. Hold the jack against a glass of water and look at the jack through the water. Slowly move the card away from the glass. You will see Jack turn and face in the opposite direction. Can you explain why?

- Write the words OXIDE and MATTER in capital letters on a piece of paper. Fill a clear glass or plastic vial with water and cap it. Hold the vial horizontally over each word, in turn. Why is one word turned upside down and not the other?

2.3 Distance and Convex Lens Images

Because you will be working with a lighted candle, do this experiment **under adult supervision**.

1. **Ask the adult** to light a candle in a dark room.
2. Hold the convex lens a meter (yard) or so from the candle.
3. The candle is on one side of the lens. Ask a partner to hold a white cardboard screen on the other side of the lens. Have your partner move the cardboard screen until a clear image of the candle appears on the screen.
4. Slowly move the lens closer to the candle. How does this affect the distance between the lens and a clear image on the screen? How does this affect the size of the image?
5. Slowly move the lens farther from the candle. How does it affect the distance between the lens and a clear image? How does this affect the size of the image?
6. Place the lens exactly two focal lengths from the candle flame. How does the distance between candle and lens compare with the distance between lens and image? How does the image's size compare with that of the candle flame?

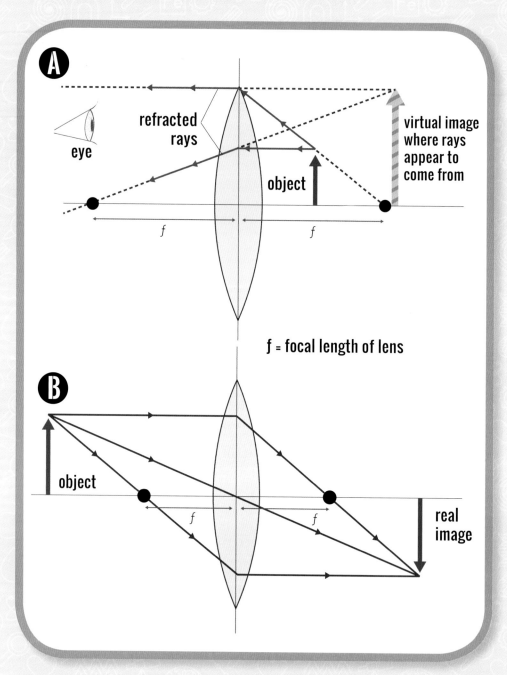

A

refracted rays

eye

object

virtual image where rays appear to come from

f

f

f = focal length of lens

B

object

f

f

real image

Figure 11. a) A magnifying glass produces enlarged virtual images when it is less than one focal length from the object. b) If the object is more than one focal length from the lens, the image is real.

7. Next, place the lens less than one focal length from the candle flame. You will not be able to capture a real image on the screen. Look at the candle flame through the lens when it is half a focal length from the candle. What do you see? How does the size of the flame's image compare with the size of the flame? Could this be a virtual image?

8. Figure 11a shows how images are formed when the object is less than one focal length from the convex lens. As you can see, all such images will be larger than the object. Figure 11b shows how real images form when an object is more than a focal length from the lens.

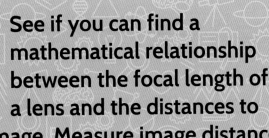

FOR A SCIENCE **IDEA** FAIR PROJECT

See if you can find a mathematical relationship between the focal length of a lens and the distances to object and image. Measure image distance from the focal point on its side of the lens and the object distance from the focal point on its side of the lens.

2.4 The Science of a Concave Mirror

THINGS YOU WILL NEED:

- **an adult**
- concave mirror (a magnifying shaving or makeup mirror is satisfactory)
- window with a view
- a partner
- sheet of white cardboard (a screen) or a sheet of white paper taped to cardboard
- ruler or meter stick or yardstick
- metal-cutting shears
- coffee can
- white paper
- dark room
- two-slit frame you used in Experiment 1.5
- flashlight

Concave mirrors are saucer-shaped. You probably have a concave mirror in your home. Makeup or shaving mirrors are concave.

1. Hold a concave mirror close to your face. You will see a magnified image. Do you think the image is real or virtual? What makes you think so?

2. Hold a concave mirror near a wall opposite a window. Ask a partner to hold a sheet of white cardboard (a screen) about a meter (yard) in front of the mirror. Turn the mirror toward the window. Move it until it reflects a clear, sharp image of the view through the window onto the screen. What do you notice about the image? Do you think the image is real or virtual? Measure the distance from the center of the mirror to the image. Record that length.

Since the image is formed by light from distant objects, the rays from those objects must be essentially parallel when they reach the mirror. The focal length of a concave mirror is the distance from the center of the mirror to the focal point. This is the point where parallel rays are brought together. Every point on the image is formed from parallel rays that come from every point on the distant objects seen in the image. Therefore, the distance you recorded is the focal length of the mirror. You will need the focal length in the next experiment.

3. To see how a concave mirror forms an image, **ask an adult** to use metal-cutting shears to cut a section about 5 cm (2 in) by 10 cm (4 in) from the side of a coffee can. The shiny concave inside surface of the can will serve as a two-dimensional concave mirror.

4. Stand the concave reflecting surface on a sheet of white paper in a dark room. Hold the two-slit frame you used in Experiment 1.5 about 10 cm (4 in) in front of the concave piece of metal.

5. Move a flashlight around in front of the two slit mask until you get two reasonably sharp rays that strike the concave surface. Notice how these reflected rays come together in front of the mirror. The same thing happens when light rays strike a concave mirror, except that it happens in three dimensions instead of two.

2.5 Distance and Concave Mirror Images

THINGS YOU WILL NEED:

- **an adult**
- matches
- candle and candle holder
- dark room
- concave mirror
- a partner
- white cardboard or white paper taped to cardboard
- ruler or meter stick or yardstick

Because you will be working with a lighted candle, do this experiment **under adult supervision**.

1. **Ask the adult** to light a candle in a dark room.

2. Hold a concave mirror a meter (yard) or so from the candle. Ask a partner to hold a white cardboard screen in front of the mirror. Have your partner move the screen until a clear image of the candle appears on the screen.

3. Slowly move the mirror closer to the candle. How does this affect the size of the image? How does it affect the distance between the mirror and the image?

4. Slowly move the mirror farther from the candle. How does this affect the size of the image? How does it affect the distance between the mirror and the image?

5. Place the mirror exactly two focal lengths from the candle flame. Where is the image? How does the size of the image compare with the size of the candle flame?

6. Next, place the mirror half a focal length from the candle flame. You will not be able to capture a real image on the

screen. But look at the candle flame you see in the mirror. How does the size of the flame's image compare with the size of the flame? Could this be a virtual image?

Figure 12a shows how images are formed when the object is less than one focal length from a concave mirror. As you can see, all such images will be larger than the object. Figure 12b shows how real images form when an object is more than a focal length from the mirror. Will all these images be smaller than the object?

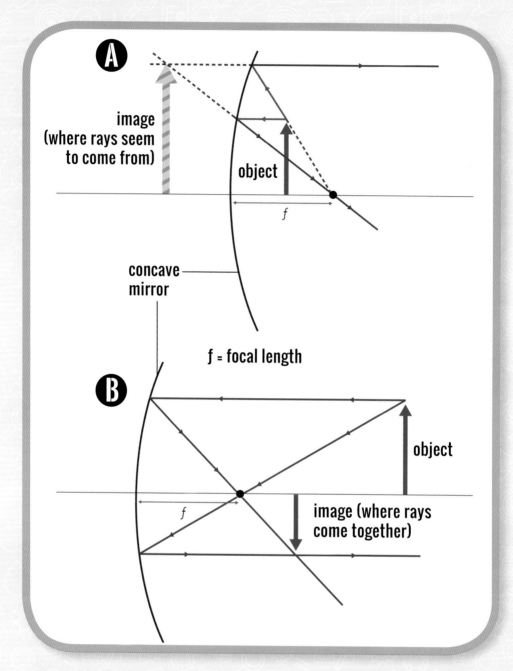

Figure 12. Images are formed by a concave mirror. a) A virtual image appears when an object is less than one focal length from the mirror. b) Real images are formed when objects are more than one focal length from the mirror.

See if you can find a mathematical relationship between the focal length of a concave mirror and the distances to object and image. Measure both image distance and object distance from the focal point of the mirror.

Investigate convex mirrors. What kind of images do they form? Where are convex mirrors used? Why not use concave or plane (flat) mirrors there?

Chapter 3

The Colors in White Light

Have you ever held a prism in a stream of light and seen the separation of colors in white light? Or perhaps you have sprayed water from a hose on a sunny day to see a rainbow appear in the water droplets? Ordinary white light can be separated into all the colors you see in a rainbow—from red to violet. There are colors beyond the red (infrared) and beyond the violet (ultraviolet), but we can't see them. Some animals can see into the infrared or ultraviolet, but our vision is limited to a shorter range of color. What they see we can only imagine.

We see colors because of cells in the retinas at the back of our eyes. It is these cells that respond to light and send nerve impulses to the brain where we actually see. The front of each eye serves as a lens that forms images on the retinas. There are two kinds of cells that respond to light. Cone cells, located near the center of our retinas, can distinguish colors. Rod cells, which are along the edges of our retinas, respond to light but not to colors. Rod cells are the cells you use to see in dimly lighted rooms such as a theater.

One theory of color vision suggests that we have three types of cone cells. One type responds to blue light, another type responds to green light, and a third type responds to red light. Blue, green, and red are the three primary colors for light. As you will see in the next experiment, all the other colors, including white, can be obtained by mixing these three primary colors in different amounts.

3.1 Primary Colors of Light

THINGS YOU WILL NEED:

- straight popsicle sticks from a crafts or hobby store
- glue
- masking tape or black tape
- red, blue, and green light filters (see Appendix for sources)
- clear light bulb with a straight-line filament
- socket for light bulb
- clay
- black cardboard or cardboard box lined with black paper
- white paper
- mirrors

1. To experiment with the three primary colors, you can start by building a square frame from popsicle sticks and glue as you did in Experiment 1.5. Add two popsicle sticks to the frame as shown in Figure 13a. Cover the three open spaces between the sticks with red, blue, and green light filters (Figure 13b). Cut narrow strips of masking or black tape to fasten the colored filters to the popsicle sticks.

2. Stand the frame upright a few centimeters (inches) in front of a clear light bulb that has a straight-line filament. A lump of clay can be used to support the frame. Be sure the filament is vertical as shown in Figure 13c. Fold a wide strip of black cardboard to place over the light bulb to screen it from your eyes, or mount the bulb inside a cardboard box lined with black paper. Be sure that all sides of the cardboard are at least 10 cm (4 in) from the bulb.

3. Lay a sheet of white paper in front of the frame to display the colors. Use mirrors to reflect colored beams and mix

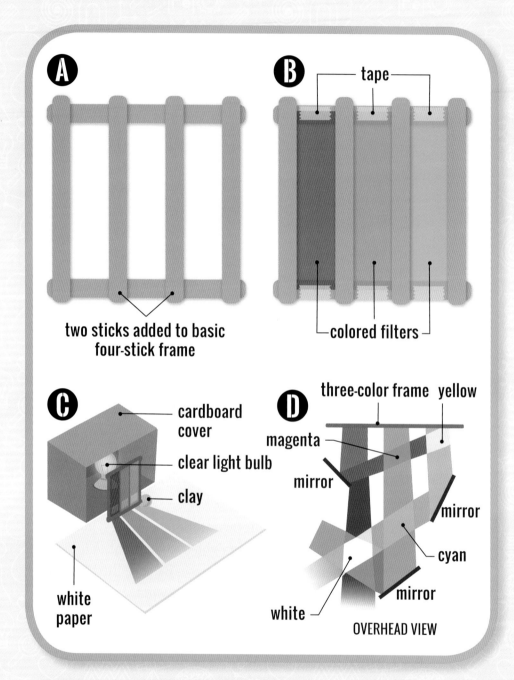

A two sticks added to basic four-stick frame

B tape — colored filters —

C cardboard cover — clear light bulb — clay — white paper

D three-color frame   yellow   magenta   mirror   mirror   cyan   mirror   white   OVERHEAD VIEW

Figure 13. a) Two sticks are added to the basic frame. b) This frame has three colored filters—red, green, and blue. c) Shining white light through the filters produces the three primary colors of light. d) Use mirrors to mix (add) colors.

(overlap) the colored lights as shown in Figure 13d. The color you obtain by mixing red and green light is yellow. The mixture may be more orange than yellow, but you can vary the intensity of a color by tilting the mirror. You should not have any difficulty producing yellow by mixing green and red.

Mixing red and blue will produce magenta. (You might call it deep pink or purple.) Mixing blue and green results in cyan, which you might call bluish green or aqua. By mixing all three primary colors you can produce white light.

3.2 Giving Shadows Color

1. Set up this experiment in the same way as you did Experiment 3.1. Use a small lump of clay to support a thin stick. Place it near the blue light filter. Use mirrors to reflect colored light.

2. Can you give the stick's dark shadow a green stripe? Can you give it a red stripe? How can you give it red, green, and yellow stripes? How about a white stripe?

3. Move the stick in front of the red filter. Can you give the dark shadow a green stripe? Can you give it a blue stripe? How can you give it blue, green, and cyan stripes?

4. Move the stick in front of the green filter. Can you give the dark shadow a blue stripe? Can you give it a red stripe? Can you give it blue, red, and magenta stripes?

Look inside and outside for colored shadows, such as the blue shadows often seen on snow. There are many. Try to explain why they have the colors they do.

3.3 Reflected Light of Colored Objects

Have you ever noticed the color of objects under the sodium vapor (yellow) lights often found in parking lots? Or have you noticed how objects take on a pinkish glow when bathed by the light of the setting sun?

1. Set up this experiment in the same way you did for Experiment 3.1. Let the three colored beams fall on a sheet of white paper.

   Colored objects reflect only certain colors of light to your eyes. An object with only red pigment or dye reflects only red light. It absorbs all the other colors in white light. As a result, it appears red. What colors found in white light would you expect a yellow object to reflect? A magenta object? A cyan object?

2. Lay a white square on the beam that comes through the red filter. What color does it appear to have? Can you explain why?

3. Repeat the experiment with the white square in the blue and green beams. What color does it appear to have in the blue light? In the green light? Can you explain why?

4. Repeat the experiment for each colored square in each colored beam. Try to explain why they appear as they do in each of the colored beams. Bear in mind that the papers may have pigments or dyes of more than one color. As a result, they may reflect more than one color.

Seeing Colors

When you look at a yellow object, the cone cells that respond to red and green light are both stimulated, which causes you to see yellow. Similarly, magenta objects stimulate the cone cells sensitive to red light and the cone cells that respond to blue light. A cyan material causes both the cone cells sensitive to blue light and the cone cells sensitive to green light to send impulses to the brain.

How can you show that some animals can see colors that humans can't? How can you show that some animals are color blind?

How can you test to see if someone is color blind? Are more men than women color blind?

3.4 White Light and Complementary Colors

Complementary colors are colors that when added together, produce white light. For example, the complementary color of blue light is yellow light. (Yellow contains both green and red light.) Consequently, if yellow light is added to blue light, we can expect to see white light.

1. To see if this is true, use glue and popsicle sticks to build a frame like the one in Figure 14a.

2. When the glue is dry, tape a blue filter over one opening and two yellow filters over the other as shown in Figure 14b. (The light through two yellow filters will be about the same intensity as the light through one blue filter.)

3. Set up this experiment in the same way you did for Experiment 3.1 using this new frame.

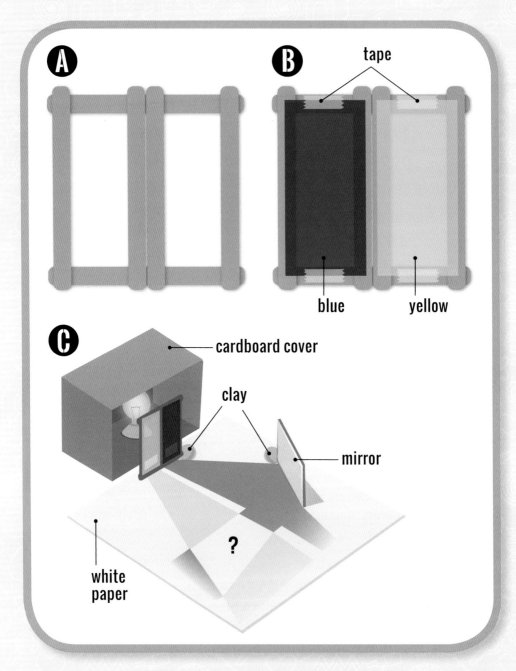

Figure 14. a) Make a two-window frame from six sticks. b) Cover one opening with a blue filter; cover the other with two yellow filters. c) **Add** (mix) the two colors. Can you get white light?

4. Use a mirror to add blue to yellow or yellow to blue as shown in Figure 14c. Can you produce white by adding these two colors together?

5. What do you think is the complementary color of green light? Remove the filters on the frame. Replace them with a green filter and two filters with the color you think is green's complementary color. Then see if you can produce white light by adding them together.

6. What do you think is the complementary color of red light? Remove the filters on the frame. Replace them with a red filter and one filter with the color you think is red's complementary color. Then see if you can produce white light by adding them together.

IDEA FOR A SCIENCE FAIR PROJECT

What are the complementary colors for the pigments that artists use? Compare and contrast complementary colors for pigments and for light.

3.5 Colors in Combination

1. Set up this experiment in the same way you did for Experiment 3.1. Let the three colored beams (blue, red, and green) fall on a sheet of white paper.

2. Hold a cyan filter in front of the red filter. What color, if any, comes through both filters?

   Now hold the cyan filter in front of the blue filter. What color, if any, comes through both filters?

   Hold the cyan filter in front of the green filter. What color, if any, comes through both filters?

3. Hold a yellow filter in front of the red filter. What color, if any, comes through both filters?

   Next, hold the yellow filter in front of the blue filter. What color, if any, comes through both filters?

   Hold the yellow filter in front of the green filter. What color, if any, comes through both filters?

4. Hold a magenta filter in front of the red filter. What color, if any, comes through both filters?

   Next, hold the magenta filter in front of the blue filter. What color, if any, comes through both filters?

   Hold the magenta filter in front of the green filter. What color, if any, comes through both filters?

   How can you explain the results of these experiments?

5. Replace the three-color frame with a two-color frame that has a cyan and a magenta filter.

6. Hold a yellow filter in front of the magenta filter. What color, if any, comes through both filters?

    Hold the yellow filter in front of the cyan filter. What color, if any, comes through both filters?

    Finally, hold a cyan filter in front of the magenta filter. What color, if any, comes through both filters?

    How can you explain the results of these experiments?

7. What color, if any, would you expect to see through a combination of three filters—cyan, yellow, and magenta? Try it! Were you right?

3.6 Light Through Colored Filters

THINGS YOU WILL NEED:

- dark room
- clear light bulb with straight-line filament
- socket for light bulb
- diffraction grating
- red, green, blue, cyan, yellow, and magenta light filters

You can use a diffraction grating to analyze the light that comes through a light filter. A diffraction grating will separate light into whatever colors it contains. For example, it will separate white light into all the colors from violet to red. You can use it as a tool to see what colors come through the various light filters you have used.

1. In a dark room, turn on a clear light bulb with a straight-line filament. Turn the bulb so the filament is vertical. Hold a diffraction grating in front of one eye. The light coming through the grating will be spread out into bright spectra (rainbows) that can be seen on either side of the bright filament. (You may have to turn the grating 90 degrees to see the colors.) If you look well to the side, you will see several spectra on either side of the filament seen through the grating.

2. Hold a light filter in front of the grating. You will see that only certain parts of the white light spectrum come through the filter. What part or parts (colors) of the white light spectrum come through each of the following filters: red, blue, green, cyan, magenta, yellow? What part or parts of the spectrum do the filters remove?

   How does this experiment help you understand what you saw in Experiment 3.4?

Try This for Fun

- Use crayons to draw a red R and a blue B on a sheet of white paper. Ask a friend what she thinks she will see if she looks at the letters through a red filter. Is your friend surprised when she can see the B and not the R? Can you explain why she sees a black B and no R (or a very faint R).

Use a diffraction grating to analyze the light from various light sources such as fluorescent bulbs, sodium vapor lamps, neon lights, candlelight, and so on.

Chapter 4

The Properties of Light

What moves faster than anything in the universe? If you said "light," you are correct! The speed of light is faster than everything else. To explain the properties of light, two theories, or models, were developed by early scientists. One model, advocated by Sir Isaac Newton (1642–1727), "pictured" light as a stream of tiny particles. Newton demonstrated that particles bouncing off smooth surfaces behaved like light reflecting from a mirror. He also showed that particles entering water were refracted.

A second model, championed by Christiaan Huygens (1629–1695), described light as wavelike. He was able to show that light had properties similar to the much larger waves seen in water.

In this chapter, you will examine both models of light. Attention will focus on properties that can be explained by assuming that light is wavelike.

4.1 Particles and Light

THINGS YOU WILL NEED:
- a tennis ball or rubber ball
- smooth floor with lines such as a tile or wood floor, not one that is carpeted

Can we explain light by thinking of it as a stream of particles traveling at a very high speed?

1. You can explore that idea by using a ball to represent a light wave. Roll a tennis or rubber ball against a wall. Bounce it off a floor. Is the ball's angle of incidence approximately the same as its angle of reflection?

   Newton used particles to explain the refraction of light. As you know, light refracts when it passes from one substance, such as air, into another, such as water or glass. Newton believed that when a particle of light traveling through air gets very close to a substance like water or glass, the substance pulls on the particle. This causes it to bend as it enters the substance. Once inside the substance, it moves in a straight line at constant speed because it is pulled equally in all directions. As light particles leave the substance and reenter air, they are pulled again, which causes their path to change again.

2. You can use an analogy to see how Newton's model works. Roll a ball that represents a particle of light along the floor. As it is about to cross a line that represents the surface of a material such as glass, give it a gentle push toward the line. Then just after it crosses another line representing the other side of the glass, give it another light push toward the line it just crossed. As you can see, the ball's path is similar to

the path followed by the light ray that you plotted as it passed through water in Experiment 1.7.

When you gave the ball a push as it entered the "substance," its speed increased. When you gave the ball a push as it left the "substance," its speed decreased. According to this model, light should go faster in water and glass than it does in air.

Particle Model Test

In 1849, Armand Fizeau (1819–1896), a French scientist, measured the speed of light in air. He found it to be approximately 300,000 kilometers per second (km/s) or 190,000 miles per second (mi/s). In 1862, another Frenchman, Jean Foucault (1819–1868), measured the speed of light in water and found it to be about 225,000 km/s (140,000 mi/s). Scientists recognized that something was wrong with the particle model of light. When light enters water, its speed does not increase, it actually decreases. The same is true of glass. The speed of light in glass is about 200,000 km/s (124,000 mi/s).

4.2 Waves and Light

To observe the similarity between light and water waves, you will need a clear glass dish or plastic box at least 20 cm (8 in) wide. A sturdy plastic box or a glass baking dish with a smooth flat bottom will be fine.

1. Put the dish or box under a single ceiling light bulb. Support the container at each end with chairs or small tables as shown in Figure 15a. Light will shine through the container and onto the floor beneath. When you are sure the pan is level, add water to a depth of about 1.5 cm (0.5 in).

2. Place a large sheet of white paper on the floor under the pan. It will serve as a screen for viewing waves.

Waves and Reflection

3. To make a wave, dip your finger into the water. Watch the wave's image move along the paper. Does the wave reflect when it reaches the walls of the pan? To prevent unwanted

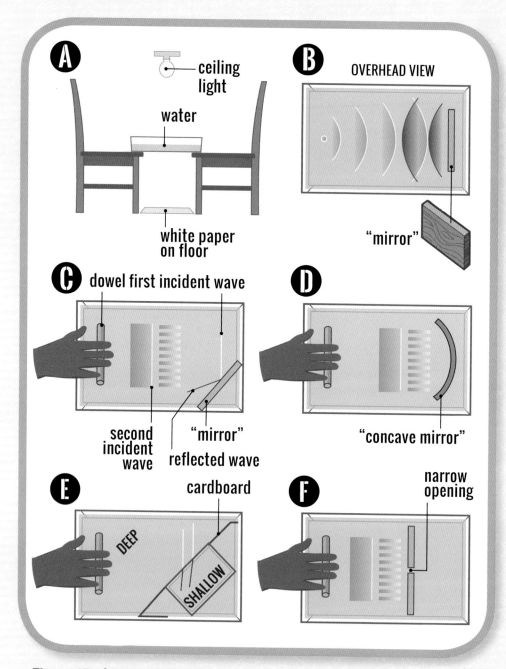

A ceiling light
water
white paper on floor

B OVERHEAD VIEW
"mirror"

C dowel first incident wave
second incident wave
"mirror"
reflected wave

D "concave mirror"

E cardboard
DEEP
SHALLOW

F narrow opening

Figure 15. a) Set up the container and light. b) View the incident wave (white) and reflected wave (brown). c) Compare angles of incidence and reflection. d) Waves are reflected by a "concave mirror." e) Refraction of waves is shown with incident waves (white) and refracted waves (brown). f) Diffraction of waves.

reflections in the next few experiments, line the walls of the pan with strips of soft cloth.

4. To look more closely at the reflection of water waves, let a flat piece of wood represent a mirror. Stand the "mirror" near one end of the pan. Dip your finger into the water at the other end of the pan. The wave you make represents light waves coming from a point of light. What happens when the wave hits the "mirror"? Where does the reflected wave seem to be coming from (Figure 15b)? Is it from where the "image" of the point of light should appear to be? What happens to the location of the "image" as you move the "point of light" closer to the "mirror"?

5. To see how the angles of incidence and reflection compare, place the "mirror" across the corner of the pan (Figure 15c).

6. Make a straight wave by gently rolling a wooden dowel along the bottom of the pan. Try not to jiggle the pan as you do this. Rolling it just a very short distance will make a satisfactory wave. The straight wave you see can represent a huge number of parallel rays moving toward the "mirror." Compare the angle at which the wave hits the "mirror" with the angle at which it is reflected. Do they appear to be equal? What happens if you change the angle by turning the "mirror"?

7. Make a concave "mirror" by putting a piece of stiff coat hanger wire into a length of rubber tubing. Bend the tubing to make a concave "mirror" (Figure 15d).

8. If you make a straight wave with the wooden dowel, can you predict how the reflected wave will look? Try it. Did you predict correctly? Remember, the straight wave represents a large number of parallel rays. Where is the "mirror's" focal point?

9. Use your finger to make waves from a "point of light" more than a focal length from the "mirror." Where does its "image" form? If you put the "point of light" less than one focal length from the "mirror," where is the "image"? What kind of "image" is it?

How can you make waves from a "point of light" change into parallel rays (straight waves) after they are reflected from the "mirror"?

Refraction and Waves

To see how waves are refracted, you need to change the speed at which the wave travels. (Remember Foucault found light moved slower in water and in glass.) You can do this by having the wave travel from deep water into shallow water.

10. Place a stack of two or three glass plates about 10–12 cm (4–5 in) square near the center of the pan. You could use a thin plastic sandwich box filled with water. Add water until the glass or box is covered with a shallow layer of water. Then make a straight wave with the dowel. You will see the wave move slower in the shallow water.

11. Turn the glass or box so that the wave hits the shallow water at an angle. Stand pieces of cardboard at the ends of the shallow region (Figure 15e). The parts of the wave that do not enter the shallow water will be reflected away. Does the wave bend when it enters the shallow water? Can a wave model explain the refraction of light?

Diffraction of Light

There is another property of light that you haven't seen yet. It is called diffraction. You can see waves diffract in the same container you have used to see waves reflect and refract.

12. Stand two flat pieces of wood upright in the pan. Leave a small opening between them as shown in Figure 15f. Send a straight wave toward the opening. What happens to the part of the wave that passes through the opening? What happens if you make the opening wider? Narrower? Is the result similar if you use a "point of light"?

IDEA FOR A SCIENCE FAIR PROJECT

Investigate ripple tanks— larger, more elaborate versions of the setup you built. Then build one and use it to experiment with waves.

4.3 What Is Diffraction?

The spreading out of waves as they pass through a narrow opening or around a corner is called diffraction. If light consists of waves, we might expect to see light diffract (spread out) as it passes through a narrow opening or around a corner. Can you detect such an effect with light?

1. To find out, **ask an adult** to light a candle in a dark room.

2. Stand several feet from the candle flame. Hold two popsicle sticks or tongue depressors in front of one eye. Hold the sticks vertically and ever so slightly apart (almost together) as you look at the candle flame through the narrow slit. Does the light spread out as it passes through the slit? Can you see bands of color in the light? What happens when you widen the slit? When you make the slit even narrower?

3. For a better view of light being diffracted, use a clear light bulb with a straight-line filament. Arrange the bulb so that the filament is vertical. Hold the two popsicle sticks parallel to the filament as you look at the glowing filament through the narrow slit. Notice the colored bands. Which light is diffracted more, blue light or red light?

4. A diffraction grating has many slits that are very narrow. An inexpensive grating has more than 5,000 slits per centimeter. This means the slits are less than 0.002 mm wide. Because the slits are so narrow, the diffracted light is widely spread.

   Hold a diffraction grating in front of one eye as you look at the light from a vertical straight-line filament in a clear bulb. You will see a rainbow of colors (a spectrum) that appears to be to either side of the light. (It is actually on your retina.) Which color is diffracted more, red or blue? (The slits need to be parallel to the line filament so you may need to rotate the grating 90 degrees.)

   You may see another one or two spectra further out on each side. In between the spectra, you see nothing because the crests and troughs of the light waves cancel one another.

Find a way to measure the wavelengths of light of different colors using a diffraction grating. Assume the grating has 5,000 slits per centimeter.

4.4 Polarized Light

Polarized Light and Light Waves

The diffraction of light offers good evidence for the wavelike nature of light. In fact, it is possible to measure the wavelength of light. Such measurements show that the wavelength of visible light is very small. It varies from about 400 nm (0.0004 mm) in deep violet light to 750 nm (0.00075 mm) in the deep red. One nm (nanometer) is one billionth of a meter.

We can represent a light wave like a water wave (Figure 16a). However, unlike a water wave, a light wave can oscillate (move back and forth) in any direction, not just up and down. Figure 16b shows an end-on view of a light wave. The arrows show a few of the many directions that a light wave can oscillate.

Sunlight reflected from water or glass is polarized. This means that the reflected light oscillates mostly vertically or horizontally as shown in Figures 16ci and 16cii. The amount of the light that is polarized depends on the angle of incidence.

Light is also polarized by some crystals, including a thin film known as Polaroid, which is its trade name. Polaroid transmits light waves that oscillate along only one of their many possible axes. The long thin crystals in Polaroid absorb some of the light to form a polarized beam that may be polarized vertically (Figure 16di) or horizontally (Figure 16dii). If two Polaroid crystals are at right angles to each other, very little light will get through (Figure 16diii).

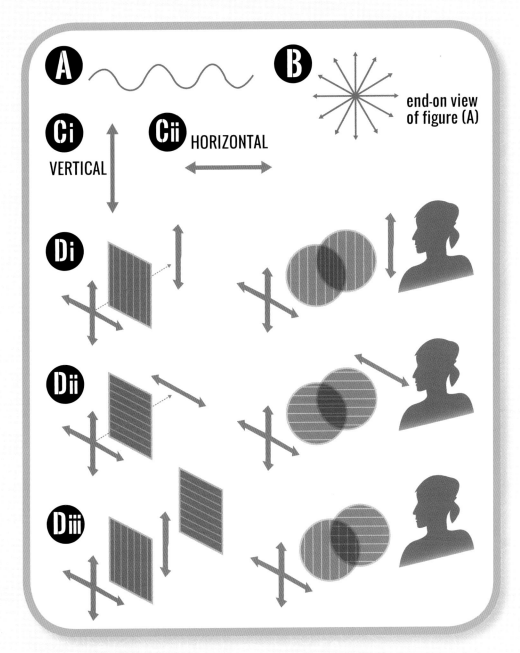

Figure 16. a) Side view of a water wave or light wave. b) End-on view of the many ways a light wave can oscillate. c) End-on view of light wave oscillating in only i) a vertical direction; ii) a horizontal direction. di) Two Polaroid sheets with parallel vertical axes allow polarized light to pass though. dii) Two Polaroid sheets with parallel horizontal axes allow polarized light to pass through. diii) Two Polaroid sheets with perpendicular axes allow polarized light to pass through the first sheet, but very little light will pass through the second sheet. It will absorb the polarized light.

The crystals act something like regularly spaced trees in an apple orchard. If you try to run between the rows of trees carrying a long stick, you can do so if you hold the stick so it points up (vertically). If you carry the stick sideways, you can't get through the trees. Polaroid works in much the same way. It allows light waves that oscillate in one direction to pass, while absorbing light that oscillates in other directions.

1. For a hands-on feel for polarized waves, you will need a long piece of rope—an old clothesline works well. (Don't use new, stiff clothesline; it must be flexible.) Tie one end of the rope to a post or have a partner hold it. With the rope slightly slack, move your hand up and down to generate waves that are polarized vertically as shown in Figure 17a.

2. Next, move your hand side to side quickly to generate waves that are polarized horizontally as seen in Figure 17b.

3. Spin your hand in a small circle the way you would if you were turning a jump rope. If you spin fast enough, you can produce several wavelengths between you and the post. These are nonpolarized waves (Figure 17c). They oscillate in all directions.

4. To make a model of what happens when light passes through Polaroid, **ask an adult** to cut a large slot in a thick sheet of cardboard. Thread the rope through the slot. Have a partner hold the cardboard firmly in place as you use the clothesline rope to send nonpolarized waves through the slot. The slotted cardboard corresponds to the Polaroid used to polarize light waves. When your partner holds the cardboard so the slot is vertical, only vertical waves will get through the slit. If your partner holds the cardboard so the slot is horizontal, only horizontal waves will get through the slit.

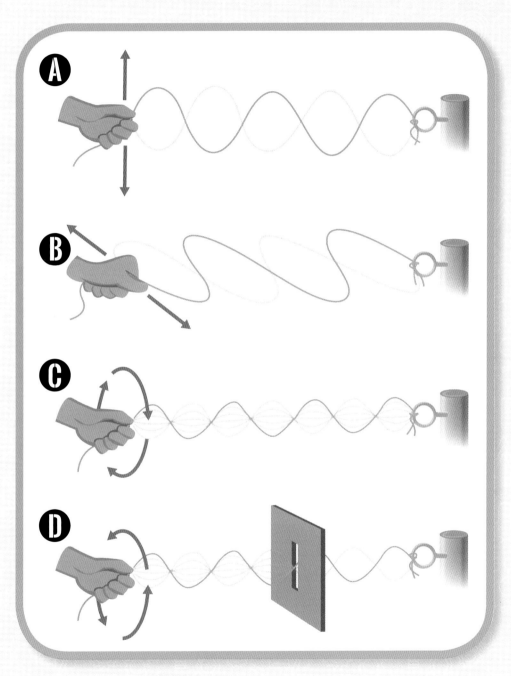

Figure 17. a) A vertically polarized wave on a clothesline. b) A horizontally polarized wave on a clothesline. c) A nonpolarized wave on a clothesline. d) Polarizing a nonpolarized wave on a clothesline.

4.5 Polarized Light and Reflection

1. Do this experiment in a dark room. Place the black side of an empty plastic CD case in front of a clear light bulb that has a straight-line filament. Be sure the filament is horizontal and parallel to the surface of the CD case.

2. Look at the light reflected from the black surface through a Polaroid sheet or the lens in a pair of polarized sunglasses.

3. Rotate the Polaroid sheet or lens. Does the intensity of the reflected light change? You will probably find the dimming is greatest when the angle of reflection is 35 to 40 degrees. Can you entirely eliminate the reflected light with the Polaroid sheet or lens?

4. Replace the plastic with a smooth metal surface such as a metallic mirror or aluminum foil. Can you reduce the intensity of the reflected light by looking at the light through a Polaroid sheet or lens that you rotate? If not, what does this tell you?

4.6 Light from the Sky

1. To answer this question, look at a blue sky about 90 degrees from the sun through a Polaroid sheet or the lens of a pair of polarized sunglasses. Slowly turn the lens or Polaroid sheet. Does the intensity of the light change?

2. Next, look at the sky closer to the sun through the same Polaroid filter. **Never look directly at the sun. It can damage your eyes**. Is the light that comes from points closer to the sun as polarized as the light you examined before? How can you tell?

4.7 Scattering Sunlight

THINGS YOU WILL NEED:

- clear drinking glass
- water
- nondairy powdered creamer
- dark room
- a partner
- flashlight
- Polaroid sheet or polarized sunglasses

1. Nearly fill a clear drinking glass with water. The water represents Earth's atmosphere. Add a pinch of nondairy powdered creamer and stir. The powder represents tiny particles—air molecules and dust—in Earth's atmosphere. These particles scatter sunlight. They absorb light and then release it, not just toward Earth, but in all directions. Scattering occurs chiefly with short wavelengths. Blue light is scattered ten times more than red light, which explains why the sky is blue.

2. In a dark room, have a partner shine a flashlight beam through the water (Figure 18a). If you look at the glass from the side, you will see that the water has a bluish tint due to scattered light. If you look at the light that has passed through the water, you will see that it is orange or reddish. Much of the blue light has been scattered so the remaining light consists of the longer wavelengths—red, orange, and yellow. Sunsets are red for the same reason. At the end of a day, sunlight has to pass through much more atmosphere than at midday. You can convince yourself of this by studying the drawing of the Earth, its atmosphere, and the sun's position at sunrise, midday, and sunset (Figure 18b).

3. Look at the bluish beam from the side of the glass. Hold a Polaroid sheet or the lens of a pair of polarized sunglasses in

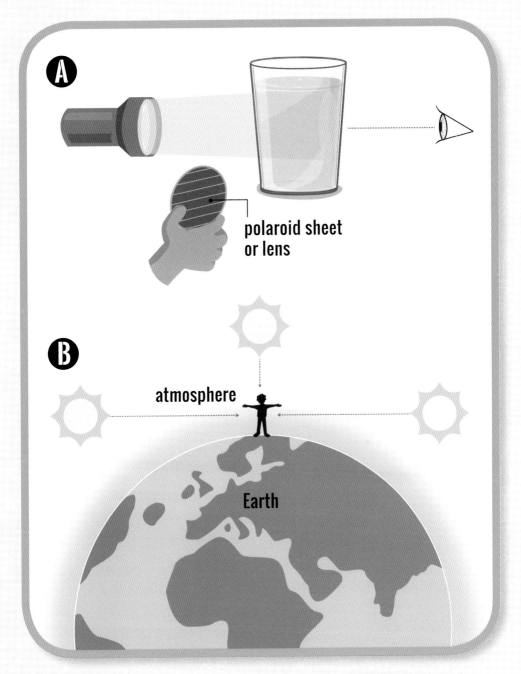

Figure 18. a) A model shows sunlight scattered by particles in the atmosphere. b) The path of sunlight through Earth's atmosphere is longest at sunrise and sunset.

front of your eye. Slowly rotate the Polaroid sheet or lens. Is the scattered light polarized? How can you tell?

4. Do you expect the unscattered light that has passed through the water (the "setting sun") to be polarized? Test your prediction using the Polaroid sheet or lens. Were you correct?

5. Can you make the "sunset" redder by stirring in more nondairy powdered creamer?

4.8 Polarized Sunglasses

THINGS YOU WILL NEED:

- book with a glossy cover
- bright light bulb
- Polaroid sheet or polarized sunglasses
- sunny day
- metal surface such as the hood of a car

1. Hold a book with a glossy cover so that it reflects light from a bright light bulb. Adjust the angle to maximize the glare.

2. Then place a Polaroid sheet or the lens of a pair of polarized sunglasses in front of your eye. Slowly rotate the Polaroid material. Is the glare reduced at a certain position of the Polaroid? Is the reflected light polarized?

3. By adjusting the book, you can vary the angle that the light strikes the book. You will find that at a particular angle practically all the reflected light is polarized. Estimate that angle. Is it about 0 degrees or 90 degrees or somewhere in between?

4. Take a pair of polarized sunglasses outside on a bright sunny day. Don't look directly at the sun as it can damage your eyes. Look for glaring light reflected from water or glass. Put on the sunglasses or look through the Polaroid sheet. Is the glare reduced? Slowly rotate the lenses or the Polaroid sheet in the reflected glare. Is the glaring light polarized? How can you tell? Does the amount that the light is polarized depend on the angle of reflection?

5. Look at light reflected from a metal surface such as the hood of a car. Examine the reflected light with your Polaroid sheet or polarized sunglasses. Is this light polarized?

4.9 A Spin on Polarized Light

THINGS YOU WILL NEED:

- polarized sunglasses
- clear jar of corn syrup (like Karo)
- bright window or a light bulb
- Polaroid sheet or the lens of another pair of polarized sunglasses
- cellophane, plastic sandwich bags, pieces of plastic, plastic containers, plastic wrap, clear plastic tape, and plastic tape holders
- glass pane such as the glass in a picture frame
- indirect sunlight

Some substances turn the plane of polarized light. For example, if polarized light that is oscillating horizontally enters a piece of cellophane, the light may be oscillating 10 degrees above or below the horizontal when it leaves the cellophane. To see the light through a second Polaroid sheet, you would have to rotate that sheet to match the rotation imposed by the cellophane.

The amount that polarized light is rotated by any material depends on the wavelength (color) of the light and the thickness of the material. As a result, you may see different colors emerge from a second Polaroid sheet as you rotate it.

1. To see some beautiful color changes produced by the rotation of polarized light, put on a pair of polarized sunglasses.

2. Place a clear jar of corn syrup (like Karo) in front of a bright window or a light bulb. Hold another Polaroid sheet or

the lens of another pair of polarized sunglasses between the light source and the syrup. Slowly rotate the Polaroid material between the light and the syrup. See the colors change as you look through your sunglasses.

3. Repeat the experiment using cellophane, plastic sandwich bags, pieces of plastic, plastic containers, plastic wrap, clear plastic tape, and plastic tape holders. Do they all rotate polarized light?

4. Find a clear plastic tape that rotates the plane of polarized light. The less expensive, yellowish tapes are more likely to work. Once you find such tape, crisscross it in various ways on a sheet of plastic. The different thicknesses will rotate different colors in polarized light by different amounts. This will enable you to see many colors at the same time when you look through your polarized sunglasses.

Try This for Fun

- Make a collage of materials that rotate polarized light on a clear plastic sheet. Support the collage above a Polaroid sheet illuminated from beneath by a bright light. Look at the collage through polarized sunglasses. Invite family and friends to view your collage. They will be glad they did.

4.10 Bubbles and Bands of Color

1. Blow some bubbles using a soap-bubble solution and the plastic-handled ring that comes with it. Look closely at the bubbles as they fall in sunlight or a well-lighted room. You will see colors in bubbles.

2. To better understand the source of these colors, place the soap-bubble solution in the refrigerator for about thirty minutes. (Cold soap films last longer.)

3. After the solution has cooled, dip the plastic ring into the solution. Then hold the ring in front of your eyes with light coming through a window behind you. As the soap film drains, it forms a wedge-shaped film that is thin at the top and wider at the bottom. You should be able to see a series of brightly colored bands. The bands at the top of the film are wider than the more closely spaced bands near the bottom of the film. You may find it helpful to look at the film through a magnifying glass. Why do these colored bands appear?

   The explanation has to do with the wavelike nature of light. The light coming from behind you is reflected at both the front and rear surfaces of the soap film. If light reflected from the rear surface is 0.5, 1.5, 2.5, 3.5, etc. wavelengths behind the light waves reflected from the front surface, the reflected waves will match. That means wave crests or wave troughs from the two reflections will join to form a bright band of light. If light reflected from the rear surface is 1, 2, 3, 4, etc. wavelengths behind the light waves reflected from the front surface, the reflected waves will cancel each other. The wave crests from one reflection will join the wave troughs from the other reflection. The result is a dark band.

Since the width of the film varies at any given time, the wavelengths of some colors will match at one thickness, while those of another color will match at a slightly different thickness. As a result, you see different colors at different places along the film. In any given color band, shorter wavelengths appear higher on the film and longer wavelengths appear lower on the film where it is thicker. A band of color is repeated each time the film's thickness increases by one wavelength.

Based on your observation, which color has the shortest wavelength? The longest wavelength?

Just before the film breaks, you will see it turn very dark near the top. This happens when the film's thickness is less than one-quarter wavelength (0.00001 mm). At this point, the two reflected waves nearly cancel one another, so very little light is seen.

Use the colors you see from a draining soap film to estimate the thickness of the film at various points. Assume blue light has a wavelength of 0.00045 mm.

Light Theories

As you have seen, a wave model can explain many properties of light. However, there are properties of light that a wave model cannot explain. For example, it cannot explain how light can cause a photoelectric cell to produce an electric current (a flow of electrons). To explain this aspect of light, we have to return to a particle model that is a modified version of Newton's theory. The particles of light in this model are regarded not as tiny bits of matter, but as tiny "bundles" of energy called photons. Still, the wave model plays a role in this theory. The energy of these photons is proportional to the frequency of the light (the number of waves per second). The shorter the wavelength, the greater the energy of the photons. Photons of blue light have more energy than photons of red light. Blue light shining on a photocell may cause electrons to flow, while red light will not. The greater the amount of blue light from a star, the greater its temperature. Scientists make use of both models of light to explain its behavior.

Chapter 5

It's Just an Illusion

Optical illusions are not only fun, they are also a way to study science! It is sometimes hard to believe, but not everything you see is really there. You have probably heard of thirsty people who think they see a lake in the desert. But the lake disappears as they approach it. They have seen a mirage. Light from a blue sky was bent (refracted) as it passed through air that differed in temperature. Because air expands when heated, warm air is less dense (lighter) than cold air. As you have seen, light bends when it passes from air into water. It also bends, although much more gradually, when it passes from cold air into hot air.

Illusions are perceptions that do not agree with reality, but the objects or images are not displaced. An artist may give the illusion of depth in a painting in several ways. He or she may paint one person smaller than another, use one object to partially hide another, add a bright color to bring an object "out of the picture," or use grays to convey a haziness we associate with distance.

Heat and Mirages

> **THINGS YOU WILL NEED:**
>
> - **an adult**
> - long (10 meters [33 feet] or more) flat wall that faces south
> - a partner
> - spoon or large key
> - clear, rectangular, plastic container about 20 cm (8 in) long and 5 cm (2 in) deep
> - metric measuring cup
> - another container
> - sugar
> - dry dairy creamer
> - glass stirring rod or straw
> - funnel
> - dark room
> - laser pointer

Mirages are displaced images. Mirages occur when light travels through layers of air that have different temperatures. You don't have to go to a desert to see mirages. You have probably seen mirages on a hot summer day while traveling along a highway. The heated highway ahead of you may have appeared to be a lake. What you were really seeing was an image of the sky. Light from the sky was refracted by the hot air above the pavement. Hot air refracts light differently than cold air. As a result, the light coming from the sky is bent so that it appears to be coming from the road. You may also have noted inverted images of cars some distance in front of you. These, too, are mirages caused by the refraction of light as it passes through air with different temperatures.

Mirages also occur when the air next to the ground is colder than the air above. In that case the light is bent downward. Objects on the horizon may appear to be above it—a phenomenon known as looming. A city's skyscrapers, normally below the horizon, may become visible under the right atmospheric conditions.

1. You can usually see a mirage on a hot summer day. You will need a south-facing flat wall that is 10 meters (33 ft) or more in length. Put your face against one end of the wall. Have a partner at the other end of the wall hold a spoon or large key close to the wall.

2. Have your partner move the object slowly toward the wall. Because of the refracted light, you will see an image of the object that appears to be on the other side of the wall.

   In the next experiment you will see that temperature differences, which change the density of a substance, really can change the path of light rays.

The Cause of Mirages

The density of air (its weight per volume) increases as light travels from the outer edges of the atmosphere to Earth's surface. Unlike the passage of light from air to water, there is a gradual bending of the light rather than a sudden change as light passes through the atmosphere. As a result, sunlight and starlight is continuously refracted as it travels through Earth's air.

Near Earth's surface, temperature differences can cause differences in the density of air. Air expands when heated, so hot air is less dense than cold air. It is differences in air temperature that created mirages like those discussed in Experiment 5.1.

3. You can create a model to show how gradual changes in density can cause light to bend gradually rather than suddenly. You will need a clear, rectangular, plastic container about 20 cm (8 in) long and 5 cm (2 in) or more deep.

4. Measure the volume of water needed to fill the container about three-quarters full. Let's assume it is 800 mL (2.7 oz). If it is, you

will need 400 mL (1.35 oz) of a concentrated sugar solution in a separate container. To prepare this solution, add 0.5 g (0.02 oz) of sugar for each milliliter of water. In the assumed case, you would add 200 g of sugar (about 14 tablespoonsful) to 400 mL (1.35 oz) of hot tap water. Stir to dissolve the sugar.

5. Pour 400 mL (1.35 oz) of hot tap water (or the volume of the sugar water) into the container. Add a pinch of a dry dairy creamer to the water and to the sugar solution. Stir to spread the solid throughout the liquids. The whitish tint to the liquids will make the light beam easier to see.

6. Next, put the spout of a funnel on the bottom of the container.

7. Slowly pour the sugar solution onto a glass stirring rod or straw into a funnel. (See Figure 19a.) Because the sugar solution is denser than the water, it will tend to remain beneath the water. But it will slowly diffuse upward creating a gradual decrease in density from the bottom to the top of the liquid.

8. Darken the room. **Under adult supervision**, shine a laser pointer into the solution near its top surface as shown in Figure 19b. You should be able to see it bend gradually as it travels along the liquid. You may also be able to make the beam bounce, as shown in Figure 19c. This will happen if the angle of refraction exceeds the critical angle for light moving from the liquid into air.

How does this experiment help in explaining mirages?

Take photographs of mirages and provide explanations of their causes.

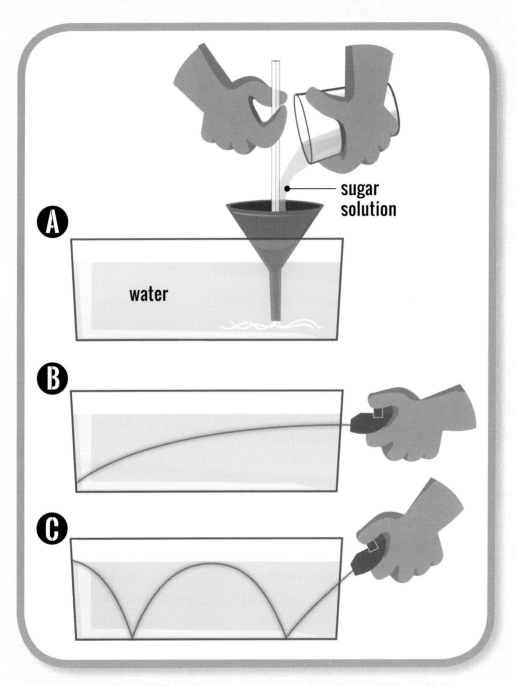

Figure 19. a) Pour a layer of sugar solution under a layer of water. b) Shine a laser beam into the cloudy liquid. Watch it bend because of differences in density. c) Watch the laser beam skip when the critical angle is exceeded.

103

5.2 **A Black and White Illusion**

THINGS YOU WILL NEED:

- **an adult**
- sunlight or brightly lit room
- copy machine
- cardboard
- pencil
- scissors
- glue
- electric drill, hand drill, or electric screwdriver
- electrical outlet

1. Look at the vertical black and white bands in Figure 20a. Find a brightly lighted place or take the book outside in sunlight. Hold the lines close to your eyes and you will see colors between the lines. Can you offer a hypothesis to explain why you see colors when none are present?

2. The circle seen in Figure 20b is known as Benham's disk. Charles E. Benham was a nineteenth-century toymaker. In 1895 Benham noticed that a black-and-white pat tern he had painted on a top produced colors when it was spinning.

3. Use a copy machine to increase the size of the circle shown in Figure 20b to a diameter of about 18–20 cm (7–8 in). Make a cardboard disk the same size as the enlarged circle.

4. Glue the enlarged black and white circle to the cardboard disk.

5. **Ask an adult** to securely attach the disk to an electric drill, hand drill, or electric screwdriver. Duct tape can be used to fasten the disk to the drill or screwdriver. If a drill with a chuck is used, a bolt can be used in place of a drill and two nuts can hold the disk in place.

   What colors do you see when the disk is spinning? Can you offer a hypothesis to explain why you see colors?

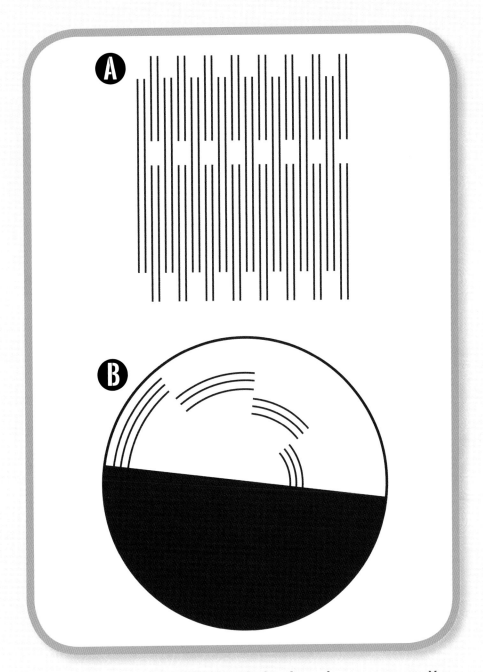

Figure 20. a) Hold these black and white lines close to your eye. You will see color between the lines. No one knows why. b) Use a copier to increase the size of the circle. What colors do you see when the disk is spinning?

Do different people see different colors when they look at the vertical bands? When they look at the spinning disk?

- Does the speed at which the disk turns affect the colors you and others see?

- Make new disks in which you replace the black and white bands with red and blue bands or with red and green bands. What colors do you see when these disks spin?

- Can you duplicate Benham's discovery by making black and white lines on a top?

5.3 The Size of the Rising Moon

A rising full moon appears much larger than it does when it is higher in the sky. Is this an illusion?

1. To find out, cut a 6-mm (1/4-inch) square in an index card.

2. Look at a full, or nearly full, moon as it rises. Put the end of a yardstick next to your eye. With the index card close to your eye, you can see a lot of sky as well as the moon through the square opening. Slide the card along the yardstick away from your eye. At what distance from your eye does the moon just fit in the square? Record this distance.

3. Later, when the moon is much higher in the sky, repeat the experiment. At what distance from your eye does the moon just fit in the square? How does this distance compare with the distance you measured when the moon was on the horizon? What do you conclude? Is the apparent size of a rising moon an illusion?

4. We are actually slightly closer to the moon when it is high in the sky than when it is rising. Can you explain why?

5. Does the direction we are looking in relation to our body have an effect on our judgment of distance and size? Some scientists think so. Look at a rising full moon as you normally would. Then lean forward so that you have to look up to see the rising moon. Does the moon appear smaller when you do this?

Some psychologists think the moon looks larger on the horizon because we see the sky as a somewhat flattened dome. To us the horizon appears farther away than the sky overhead. As a result, the moon appears larger on the horizon because we think it is farther away than when it is overhead.

FOR A SCIENCE
IDEAS
FAIR PROJECT

- Photograph the moon at as it rises and at hourly intervals until it is high in the sky. Use the photo graphs to compare the moon's size at different points in its path across the sky.

- Carry out experiments to explain why the rising moon appears to be so large.

5.4 What Is an Afterimage?

As you learned in Chapter 3, we see color because of the cone cells in our retinas. Cone cells, like muscle cells, tire with use. If you stare at one color for a long time, the cone cells sensitive to that color tire. Once tired, they do not respond as well. As a result, you may see a complementary color when you look at a white surface. Normally, white light stimulates all three types of cone cells equally, which is why we see white. However, if the cone cells sensitive to red light are tired, they will not respond as well as the other cone cells. Then the cone cells that respond to white will be those sensitive to blue and green.

1. Lay two sheets of white paper on a table that is well lighted. Place a bright red square on one of the white sheets. Stare at the red square for about 20 seconds. Then shift your gaze to the other white sheet. What color do you see on that sheet? What you see is called an afterimage. Does the afterimage have the complementary color of red light?

2. Repeat the experiment with a bright blue square. What color do you expect the afterimage to have? Were you right?

3. Repeat the experiment with a bright green square. What color do you expect the afterimage to have? Were you right?

4. Repeat the experiment three more times, first with a cyan square, then with a magenta square, and finally with a yellow square. Try to predict the color of the afterimage each time. Were you right each time?

5. If you stare at a black square for 20 seconds, what would you expect the color of its afterimage to be? Try it! Did you make the correct prediction?

5.5 More Illusions

1. Draw the following pictures on separate sheets of white paper: a fish bowl filled with clear water, a bright red fish that is smaller than the bowl, a bright green fish that is smaller than the bowl, a bright blue fish that is smaller than the bowl.

2. Stare at the red fish for 20 seconds. Then look at the picture of the fish bowl on the other white sheet. What do you see in the bowl?

3. Stare at the green fish for 20 seconds. If you then look at the picture of the fish bowl on the other white sheet, what will you expect to see in the bowl? Were you right?

4. Stare at the blue fish for 20 seconds. If you then look at the picture of the fish bowl on the other white sheet, what will you expect to see in the bowl? Were you right?

How can you make yourself see afterimages that are larger than the objects you stared at? How can you produce afterimages that are smaller than the objects you stared at? How can you explain your ability to make enlarged and shrunken afterimages?

Will afterimages seen after staring with one eye open be seen by the eye that was closed? Do an experiment to find out. What do your results tell you about afterimages?

Science Supply Companies

Arbor Scientific
PO Box 2750
Ann Arbor, MI 48106-2750
(800) 367-6695
arborsci.com

Carolina Biological Supply Co.
PO Box 6010
Burlington, NC 27215-3398
(800) 334-5551
carolina.com

Connecticut Valley Biological
   Supply Co., Inc.
82 Valley Road
PO Box 326
Southampton, MA 01073
(800) 628-7748
ctvalleybio.com

Educational Innovations, Inc.
5 Francis J. Clarke Circle
Bethel, CT 06801
(203) 748-3224
teachersource.com

Fisher Science Education
300 Industry Drive
Pittsburgh, PA 15275
(800) 955-1177
fishersci.com

Frey Scientific
80 Northwest Blvd.
Nashua, NH 03061-3000
(800) 225-3739
freyscientific.com

Nasco
901 Janesville Ave.
Fort Atkinson, WI 53538
(800) 558-9595
enasco.com/science

Products on Demand
(A good source of color filters)
108 Barnes Road
Stamford, CT 06902
(203) 322-1774
www.productsondemand.biz

Scientifics Direct
532 Main Street
Tonawanda, NY 14150
(800) 818-4955
scientificsonline.com

Ward's Science
5100 West Henrietta Road
PO Box 92912
Rochester, NY 14692-9012
(800) 962-2660
wardsci.com

Sources of Light Filters

When you are looking for light filters, try theatrical supply stores, the internet, science supply companies, and hobby stores. For example, Arbor Scientific sells a kit of six 10-in color filters (catalog # 33-0190) that has all the colors you will need for a very reasonable price. Also, Products on Demand sells Roscolene color filters (gels) at reasonable prices. Websites where color gels may be ordered include: stagelightingstore.com and djdepot.com/zprogelsh-gel-sheet-p-345.html.

Glossary

afterimage An image that remains on the retina for some time after it is no longer being viewed.

complementary colors Colors that produce white light when added together.

cone cells Cells in the center of the retina that respond to different colors in light.

convex lens A lens that is thicker in the middle and thinner around the edges. It can be used to form real images.

diffraction The spreading out of waves as they pass through a narrow opening or around a corner.

diffraction grating A device that has many narrow slits. Light that passes through it is diffracted, separating light into whatever colors it contains. For example, it will separate white light into a spectrum containing all the visible colors from violet to red.

dispersion The spreading of refracted white light into different colors, forming a spectrum. Shorter wavelengths, such as blue light, are refracted more than longer wavelengths, such as red light.

focal length The distance from the center of a convex lens or concave mirror to the focal point.

focal point The point where parallel rays are brought together by a convex lens or a concave mirror.

illusions Perceptions that do not agree with reality.

law of reflection The angle of incidence of a light ray equals its angle of reflection, and both rays lie in the same plane.

lens A shaped piece of transparent material that refracts light.

light filter A transparent material that allows only certain colors of light to pass through it. For example, a blue filter transmits only blue light. All other colors are removed.

mirages Displaced images that occur when light travels through layers of air that have different temperatures.

oscillate To move back and forth.

parallax The apparent change in an object's position compared with a more distant object when viewed from different places. Lack of parallax can be used to locate an object.

parallel light rays Light rays that are the same distance apart throughout their length. Light rays from distant objects are essentially parallel.

particle model A theory, developed originally by Isaac Newton, that views light as tiny particles.

photons Tiny "bundles" of light energy. The energy of a photon is related to wavelength. Photons of blue light have more energy than photons of red light.

pinhole image An image formed when light passes through a small hole.

polarized light Light in which the waves oscillate mostly vertically or horizontally rather than in all directions as ordinary light does.

Polaroid A material that transmits light waves that oscillate in only one plane.

primary colors Colors that may be combined to create all other colors. The primary colors of light are red, green, and blue.

real image An image formed by light rays that converge (come together). Real images can be "captured" on a screen, unlike virtual images.

reflection The bouncing of light from a surface. If the surface is smooth, an image may be seen in the reflecting surface.

refraction The change in direction of light when it passes from one substance into another. This is because light travels at different speeds in different substances.

retina A layer of cells at the back of the eye. These cells respond to light and connect to nerve cells that send nerve impulses to the brain.

rod cells Cells in the retina that respond to light—even dim light—but not to color.

virtual images Images that are formed by diverging light rays. They appear to be in positions where the light rays seem to be coming from. Such images cannot be "captured" on a screen, unlike real images.

wave model A theory that considers light to behave like waves.

Further Reading

Books

Barrett, Raymond E., and Windell Oskay. *The Annotated Build-It-Yourself Science Laboratory.* San Francisco, CA: Maker Media, 2015.

Brown, Jordan. *Science Stunts: Fun Feats of Physics.* Watertown, MA: Charlesbridge Publishing, 2016.

Buczynski, Sandy. *Designing a Winning Science Fair Project.* Ann Arbor, MI: Cherry Lake Publishing, 2014.

Clark, John O. E. *The Basics of Light.* New York, NY: Rosen Publishing, 2015.

Colson, Mary. *The Science of Light.* New York, NY: Gareth Stevens Publishing, 2016.

Harris, Tim, ed. *Physical Science.* New York, NY: Cavendish Square Publishing, 2016.

Henneberg, Susan. *Creating Science Fair Projects with Cool New Digital Tools.* New York, NY: Rosen Central, 2014.

Mercer, Bobby. *Junk Drawer Physics: 50 Awesome Experiments That Don't Cost a Thing.* Chicago, IL: Chicago Review Press, Inc., 2014.

Oxlade, Christopher. *Experiments with Sound and Light.* New York, NY: PowerKids Press, 2015.

Websites

Exploratorium
exploratorium.edu/snacks/collection/color
Check out the links to projects and experiments about light and color.

Optics for Kids
optics4kids.org/home/kids
Enjoy optical illusions as well as science project ideas about light and color.

Reeko's Mad Scientist Lab
reekoscience.com
Click on the links to experiment ideas, science news, and resources.

Index

About the Author

Robert Gardner is an award-winning author of science books for young readers. He retired from Salisbury School in Connecticut, where he chaired the science department for more than thirty years, to pursue a career as an author. He lives on Cape Cod with his wife, Patsy, and enjoys writing, biking, and doing volunteer work.